100 MINUTES
That'll change THE WAY YOU LIVE!

PEARLS OF WISDOM

Dr. L. Prakash

UNICORN

Publishers
UNICORN BOOKS Pvt. Ltd., New Delhi-110002
E-mail: unicornbooks@vsnl.com
Website: www.unicornbooks.in • www.kidscorner.in

Distributors
Pustak Mahal, Delhi
J-3/16, Daryaganj, New Delhi-110002
☎ 23276539, 23272783, 23272784 • *Fax:* 011-23260518
E-mail: info@pustakmahal.com • *Website:* www.pustakmahal.com

London Office
5, Roddell Court, Bath Road, Slough SL3 OQJ, England
E-mail: pustakmahaluk@pustakmahal.com

Sales Centre
10-B, Netaji Subhash Marg, Daryaganj, New Delhi-110002
☎ 23268292, 23268293, 23279900 • *Fax:* 011-23280567
E-mail: rapidexdelhi@indiatimes.com

Branch Offices
Bangalore: ☎ 22234025
E-mail: pmblr@sancharnet.in • pustak@sancharnet.in
Mumbai: ☎ 22010941
E-mail: rapidex@bom5.vsnl.net.in
Patna: ☎ 3294193 • *Telefax:* 0612-2302719
E-mail: rapidexptn@rediffmail.com
Hyderabad: *Telefax:* 040-24737290
E-mail: pustakmahalhyd@yahoo.co.in

© Copyright : Unicorn Books

ISBN 978-81-780-6122-1

Edition : January 2007

The Copyright © of this book as well as all matter contained herein (including illustrations) rests with UNICORN BOOKS. No person shall copy the name of the book, its title design, matter and illustrations in any form and in any language, totally or partially or in any distorted form. Anybody doing so shall face legal action and will be responsible for damages.

Printed at : Param Offsetters, Okhla, New Delhi-110020

*Dedicated to
my friend Dr. N. C. Asthana,
IPS, I.G. of Police,
who has taught me that the
written word can still inspire and
imbibe confidence, and to
my family who have stood
by me in times of crises.*

Introduction

Discover the 90/10 principle! It will change your life, I promise! What is this principle? It says that 10% of life is made up of what happens to you; 90% of life is decided by how you react to the situations. What does this mean? It means that we really have no control over 10% of what happens to us. For example, what you eventually achieve in life depends on a lot of factors including your natural abilities, your family background, the social ambience in which you grow up, how much luck favours you and so on, all of which are beyond your control. You cannot stop the train from running late. You cannot stop the traffic light from turning red when you are late. You cannot stop the boss from criticising you. Don't fret over such things. They are only the 10%. The other 90% is different. You determine the other 90%. How? By your reaction! Life in the fast-paced modern world is highly competitive, complex and stressful. Does it mean that we are condemned to succumbing to the pressures of life, wasting our time and energies in fighting things that we cannot change and becoming a victim of stress? No! Life does present many challenges and many odds stacked against you. You cannot change everything that you don't like nor can you run away from everything that does not suit you. I am not saying that you must resign yourself to your fate. What I am saying that you should make the most of the life you have got. If the pressures of life start dictating your life then you are a loser.

I want you to become a 'successful survivor'. This book radically different from the run-of-the-mill self-help and motivational books. This contains the 'top tips' that I have learnt myself in the process of surviving some great crises in life and thus speak with the authority of personal experience. This is real stuff for real people—no lectures, no empty talk, only immensely practical wisdom! How to survive against overwhelming odds in life and yet make the most of life—this is the *mool mantra* of this unique little book, all told in a uniquely humorous way through funny stories, parables and jokes. You have to read it to believe it!

DR. L. PRAKASH
M.S. (Orth.), M.Ch. (Liverpool)

Director
Institute for Special Orthopaedics, Chennai
(Former Secretary, Indian Orthopaedic Association, Joint Replacement Specialist, author of 6 professional books, 63 research papers in international journals, and holder of 42 patents)

Contents

1. Snobbery does not help   9
2. Ten asses don't make a horse   10
3. Change or perish   11
4. Present unpleasant truths pleasantly   12
5. Real life is more complex than you think   13
6. Persistence pays   14
7. Think before you speak   15
8. Don't make promises that you cannot fulfil   16
9. Sometimes you may have to compromise with the boss   17
10. The offers in your deals must be unambiguous   18
11. What matters is what can be proven   19
12. Don't put your foot in your mouth   20
13. Be extremely wary of tall claims   21
14. Not all things in life can be bargained   22
15. Be wary of self-styled consultants   23
16. Intelligent enemy vs stupid friend   24
17. One who changes with change survives   26
18. Do compete but in a healthy way   28
19. Never underestimate the capabilities of others   29
20. Avoid stubborn people, don't try to change them   30
21. If it is too good, there has to be a catch in it   31
22. Have faith, it helps   32
23. Corruption and bribes   33
24. One who grabs the opportunities shall survive   34
25. Be kind to others, it helps you too   35
26. The wonders of mutual help   36
27. Reign in your jealousy, man   37
28. When in trouble, don't seek the easy way out   38
29. An idiot can mess up everything—avoid him   39
30. You better accept Murphy's Law   40

31. Beware of all that looks too good   41
32. Keep expectations high, but not too high   42
33. Genies are for kids and not for you   43
34. It is childish to act on impulse   45
35. Don't fall into the trap of 'if he can do it, so can I'   47
36. Tangential thinking profitable thinking   48
37. If you are learning something from somebody, learn it fully   49
38. Savour the love of your loved ones before it is too late   50
39. The importance of proper data evaluation   51
40. Talent always costs money   52
41. Do not follow blindly   53
42. What not to forget   54
43. Rules for alcohol   55
44. There is no use gilding the lily   56
45. Religion and rituals   57
46. Appropriate technology —when in snow, use a ski   59
47. Tenacity and determination are keys to success · 61
48. Survivors avoid 'a holier-than-thou' person like the plague   62

49. One who invites trouble deserves it   63
50. Help only the truly deserving   64
51. The power of positive thinking   65
52. You hold your destiny   66
53. Destiny   67
54. The importance of your social obligations   68
55. If you can't lick them, join them   69
56. Don't miss the macro picture for the micro picture   70
57. Don't let stupid rules and regulations make you stupid   71
58. Look for the real McCoy; don't get fooled by red herrings   72
59. Learn to read between the lines   74
60. Impulsiveness kills   76
61. Intelligence quotient   77
62. Think before you pay in advance   78
63. In the poker of life don't play blind   79
64. Accept your limitations and be happy with them   80
65. Bad luck is bad luck, accept it   81

66. Upgrades and upgradation   82
67. Lakshmana Rekha   83
68. Selective delusions   85
69. Prepare for the indirect consequences too   87
70. Money is important, but not all that important   88
71. Confidence is good, over-confidence is bad   89
72. The value of experience   90
73. Ingenuity   91
74. Become what you think you are   92
75. Even copying demands brains   93
76. Impossible to please   94
77. Work is worship   95
78. There is always a third option   97
79. Get quickly to the crux of the matter   99
80. Use consultants, but don't let them take you for a ride   100
81. Club membership   102

82. One should take calculated risks, but not needless ones   104
83. Look for the right man for the job   105
84. When the jab slips, land a hook   106
85. Tough times don't last, tough guys do   107
86. Cut the crap   108
87. Optimal capacity   109
88. Doing a favour   110
89. Ignorance is not bliss   111
90. Value thy freedom   112
91. A cheap thing is not always a bargain   114
92. The company you keep   116
93. Smartness pays   117
94. Don't hide anything from your doctor and lawyer   118
95. At the end of everything, there is God   119
96. Kindness   120
97. A pig remains a pig   121
98. Lateral effect   122
99. Alcohol   123
100. Formal education is not the same as knowledge   124

Snobbery does not help

A crab came of age and her parents wanted her to get married. But this was no ordinary crab. She was a prim and proper crab. She was haughty too. She was a snob. "I won't marry an ordinary crab," she proclaimed. Suitors came from far and wide. And all of them, like all crabs do, walked sideways. She rejected them all. One fine day, she saw a crab that walked straight! Yes, this one walked back to front rather than side to side like other crabs. The lady was impressed and the two got married and were sent to their own crab hole. That night, the lady crab realised that this chap stank of alcohol had two broken claws and a bent pincer. But she consoled herself that she had a unique and different husband. The next morning she got a surprise when she saw her husband crawl out of the crab hole. The chap walked from side to side like any other ordinary crab. The lady was devastated. She blurted out, "But you were walking straight last night!" In a slurred voice the male crab replied, "Well baby, it is not everyday that you drink a whole bottle of rum!" The lady crab learnt it the hard way. She had to pay too high a price for snob value.

> *Snob value, thus, is a character that adds a false value to a product or act to tempt snobs who are essentially weak and foolish. To avoid snobbery is a sign of strength and wisdom.*

Snob value is putting value to irrelevant things, which appear useful but are actually worthless.

Ten asses don't make a horse

Dronacharya was the teacher who taught both, the Kauravas and the Pandavas. The princes would undergo periodic tests and examinations to assess their knowledge and skills. Yudhishthir was the eldest among the Pandava brothers while Duryodhana led the Kaurava team. Once, Guru Dronacharya asked the two teams to fill up two same sized rooms with the lightest material in the quickest time possible. The Kaurava prince immediately summoned dozens of servants and procured cartloads of straw and hay with which he proceeded to stack his room. But Yudhishthir was far too clever. He just took a couple of joss sticks and lit them in the room. He sprinkled two drops of the finest perfume too. In a matter of moments, his room was full of pleasant smell and swirls of hazy smoke.

> *It is only logical and wise that we stress more on quality in all aspects of life. That would decidedly make us happier persons.*

In our life, society teaches us that more is better. More marks than your colleague; more colour pens than your classmate; more money than your neighbour; bigger house, more cars, greater comforts, larger television, most modern PC, etc., etc. It has become a *mantra* of quantity. More and more of everything with scant regard to quality. But in the end, it is only quality that matters. In our rapid race in life and a greedy quest for more and more, we don't realise that with more and more quantity we get less and less quality.

PEARL 3
Change or perish

Three majestic Arabian camels were standing next to each other. The one to the left was the mother camel. The one to the right, standing taller and more majestic than her, was the father camel. And between the two stood a baby camel. This little camel was a curious chap. He looked up to his father and asked, "Dada, why do we have such hoofs and strangely-shaped long legs?" "So that we could run fast in the deserts without our feet sinking in the sand, sonny," replied the father. The curious baby camel was not finished. "Dada, why do we have the humps?" "Well sonny, beneath them we have the sacs that store water. We can thus live in hot deserts without water for a long long time." "Dada, why do we have such long eye lashes?" "So that we can surge ahead unperturbed by the desert storms blowing sand into our eyes!" The baby camel was a little thoughtful and then asked his final question, "But then Dada, what are we doing in Boston Zoo?"

> *Thus, we have either to acquire skills suited to our environment or change our environment to suit our skills.*

This tells us the value of skills appropriate to the environment we work in. Each skill is valuable only in a particular circumstance. You must acquire skills that suit your circumstances or move to a place where your skills would be useful. A scholar in Vedic Sanskrit has little scope in Bangalore. To survive in Bangalore, you must become a techie or else move to Kashi.

4 Present unpleasant truths pleasantly

A Managing Director in the firm looked at his budgetary allocation and found that despite living in the electronic age, a phenomenal amount of paper was consumed for inter-office memos. Each memo would be copied a dozen times with a copy marked to each department. The M.D. wanted to curtail this wastage of paper. Before taking any action, he conducted a study and found that the chief culprits were the senior-most managers who were compulsive memo writers. He realised that directly confronting the managers would eventually not serve any purpose. He decided to sugar-coat the bitter truth in a diplomatic manner. Rather than call his managers and instruct them to check their habit of sending memos, he did it by setting an example. He sent a memo to all the employees but decided to send it as an email. At the bottom was a single line **"Save our forests by conserving paper."** The main memo did not have a single word about using electronic memos instead of paper. But his pleasantly presented truth struck home and in a single month, he could clearly see the reduction in stationery bills.

> *A wise person always ensures that an unpleasant truth is presented in a pleasant manner.*

Human ego is fragile. It is incapable of bearing the burden of unpleasant truths.

When we have to correct someone or criticise someone, it has to be done in a way that it does not hurt. By being bold, forthright, and blurting out the unpleasant truth as it is, we would only stimulate resistance and anger in the listener. The purpose of correcting his mistake is not achieved. A wise man would thus couch an unpleasant truth in a pleasant manner. He would even use a redirected misdirection to prove his point. This way he would ensure that his advice is taken in the right spirit and acted upon.

PEARL 5 — Real life is more complex than you think

A scientist was evaluating the nature of grasshoppers. He set about with his experiments with a grasshopper and a measuring scale. He made a grasshopper jump and it jumped six inches. He plucked out one leg and it jumped five. One more leg plucked and it jumped only four inches. As each leg came out, it jumped lesser and lesser. Once all its six legs had been plucked out, it would not jump at all. The scientist had noted down all the conclusions one by one. Finally, he noted the results of the study: "As each leg of a grasshopper is detached, it gets deafer and deafer. And once you pluck out the last leg, it becomes stone deaf because despite repeated instructions in a loud voice, it fails to jump."

> *We live in a complex society and must realise that appearances are indeed deceptive.*

Just because two events occur together does not necessarily mean that one is because of the other or necessarily related to the other! It is essential to understand the fundamental truth that in all cases, the cause and effect can not be directly related. A wrong interpretation would surely lead to wrong conclusions as evident from the following–

1. A loaf of bread is a necessity.
2. A steam engine is an invention.
3. Necessity is the mother of invention.
4. Ergo–A loaf of bread is the mother of a steam engine!

PEARL 6

Persistence pays

One traditional form of offering prayers is to break coconuts before the image of God. When the prayers of a rich patron are answered, he may break even five hundred or a thousand coconuts. Outside a temple not far away from my house was a slab of granite that was used for coconut-breaking since centuries. One fine day, when the priest struck a coconut on it, it was the stone that split into two. Repeated cracking of coconuts had produced a stress fracture in the stone and broken it eventually!

> *Thus, a survivor would not accept a statement just because a majority of people believes in it. He does what he has to do and results eventually come to him because of his repeated and persistent efforts.*

A coconut is a hard object but a cloth is not. All we need is to go to a *dhobi ghat* and look at the washing stones. If you touch the upper surface, it would be smooth like marble or glass. Repeated hits with a wet cloth over the years has smoothened a granite stone.

Even a cloth has a certain weight but what of water? A visit to a brook or a river, and a look at the round pebbles at the riverbank would tell us that even water, which had flown doggedly over irregular and rough rocks, polishes it round and smooth.

The coconut did not say that the granite was too strong. Nor did either the cloth or the water. They continued to do what they had to do without any care for consequences. And one day the boulder cracks or a pebble smoothens up.

Think before you speak

A British Airways aircraft was about to land at London's Heathrow airport. The co-pilot initiated the landing procedure while the pilot flicked the switch on the mike and started his announcement: "We are circling Heathrow airport and awaiting landing permission which we expect shortly. The weather outside is bright and sunny. The outside temperature is nineteen degrees Celsius. I wish you all a happy landing and thank you for flying British Airways."

He then flicked the switch and turned to his co-pilot as he continued the conversation: "And the first thing I am going to do when I land is to have a pint of chilled beer and then make passionate love to the blonde long-legged air hostess who has joined us last week."

> Iyer and Iyer, have written in their classic book on cross-examination: "Never ask a question to a witness in a box, unless you definitely know what the answer is going to be!"

Unfortunately, due to some malfunction, the mike switch had remained on and his voice boomed into the entire cabin through the PA system. A visibly embarrassed long-legged blonde airhostess rushed to the cockpit to warn the pilot and stumbled in her hurry. An elderly lady who was there said softly, "Now, young lady, no need to hurry. I clearly heard him say that he was going to have the beer first."

We should not open our mouths unless we are sure of what we are going to say, who the listener is or could be, and what effect it would have on him.

Don't make promises that you cannot fulfil

An elderly man went to an optician's shop to get his eye-sight tested. Before his eye test and spectacle fitting, he asked the optician, "Can I read properly if I wear a pair of spectacles? And how long would it take?"

The optician calculated a little and said, "Half an hour for the eye test and another half for fixing the lenses on the frame. I would guess about an hour!"

The old man wanted some reassurance.

"Are you certain about the time period?"

The optician smiled, "Maybe, give or take another fifteen minutes. I will guarantee you that you would read clearly in an hour and a half, maximum."

> *A survivor thus knows his limitations and does not make promises that he cannot fulfil.*

The old man took his seat on the stool and smiled. "Well that is perfect I should say. The chaps at the adult education centre told me that it would take at least six to eight months."

One should never accept a client or make promises unless he realises what exactly the client wants.

A doctor might think that taking away the tumour, chemotherapy and radiation, to save the cancer patient's life would be the appropriate treatment. But unless he tells the patient before the start of the treatment that the tumour can recur despite best efforts, he might be left with a disappointed and angry patient.

Likewise, people in the legal profession should exercise adequate care that they only make those promises to their clients that they can deliver. Else, a customer expecting sudden literacy with reading glasses might be disappointed.

Sometimes you may have to compromise with the boss

Once there was an argument among the various body organs as to who was the big boss. The brain, as the centre of intellect, obviously wanted to be the boss. The heart insisted that it was the boss. The eyes, which saw the whole world, were also contenders for the post. While the various organs were staking their claims, the anus said in a soft voice that he too was a contender. The other body organs laughed it off and even refused to consider his proposition seriously. The anal canal was livid with rage and decided to go on strike. And once the body exit was blocked, all hell broke loose. The body was full of toxic material and it could not withstand the troubles beyond a couple of days. Eventually, they all realised that unless they acceded to the claim of the anal canal, they would all perish. So, it was made the boss.

> *There is no point in annoying an asshole when he has his hands on your neck!*

Certain realities in life have to be faced. On more than one occasion, we can find ourselves working under someone of significantly lesser intellect or talent. A survivor knows when to make a compromise and keep quiet.

Pearl 10 — The offers in your deals must be unambiguous

In an English court, a lawyer pleaded to the judge: "My Lord, it is not my client who has committed the theft. It is my client's right hand. My Lord, how can you expect my client to be punished for a crime that his right hand has done?" The judge peered through his bifocals and eyed the thief. He then pronounced his verdict: "I find the client's right hand guilty of theft and sentence it to three years' rigorous imprisonment. It is up to your client whether he accompanies his hand to the prison." A twitter of applause rose in the court hall at such an excellent judgement but that applause was short-lived, because the thief removed his false arm, placed it on the judge's table and walked away!

Never make an outrageous bet unless you are sure that the opposition would not take on it.

> *A survivor must be clear and unambiguous in the offers he makes in any deal. This would avoid unpleasant surprises at a later stage.*

I have faced this situation in real life too. I owned a mango orchard in the neighbouring state. Once, a local landlord visited me and expressed interest in buying the property. I had no special interest in selling it. The right thing for me at that moment would have been to clearly tell him that I did not want to sell the property. But I made an outrageous bet by quoting him five times the price. I knew that he knew the market value and would go away, but he surprised me by accepting the offer and paying me an advance on the spot. He had come prepared. It was a couple of months later that I came to know that the government was laying a canal irrigation system, which had to pass through that land. The government acquired it from the landlord at four times what he had paid me!

It is better to be clear and unambiguous in our offer in any deal.

PEARL 11: What matters is what can be proven

Once somebody was charged with murder. His brother was conversing with his lawyer who was arguing for bail. There was a drunken brawl in which the accused had hacked a farmer to death. The accused had spent thirty-two days in prison. I could hear the conversation between the lawyer and the client.

Lawyer: Can you get me a sworn affidavit from the village administrative officer that the opponent burnt your crops?

Client : But Sir, the deceased did not burn our crops.

Lawyer: I am not asking you if crops were burnt. I am asking you if you can get a sworn affidavit.

> *A survivor knows that what eventually matters is what can be proven.*

Client: If I pay some money, I can get it I guess.

Lawyer: Leave the rest to me.

When his turn came, the lawyer argued: "My Lord, this is a crime of passion. This has happened in a fit of anger. The deceased had burnt the crops which the accused had just harvested. The accused approached the victim, a fight ensued and in a fit of anger one person lost his life. My client is fifty-one years old, diabetic and suffers from kidney failure. He had no police record and is languishing in the prison for the last thirty-two days. He may please be released on bail, My Lord........

After his client got the bail, they conversed in whispers.

Client: But my brother has eight cases pending against him!

Lawyer: The judge does not know.

Client: My brother neither has diabetes nor kidney problem!

Lawyer: I know. You better get some medical certificates ready, just in case!

Don't put your foot in your mouth

I had a personal experience, which was such an embarrassing moment that I simply cannot forget it. I was getting inundated with unsolicited calls and messages from various banks that offered credit cards and home loans. The fact that I already owned a home and was a proud possessor of half a dozen gold and platinum cards did not seem to matter at all to these banks who persisted in making calls to me in all types of voices, and sending salesmen and women of all shapes and sizes to my home and office.

Once, a visitor sent her visiting card in. One look at her visiting card interrupted me in the middle of a busy schedule and my blood pressure shot sky high because it was from one of the banks that had been hounding and harassing me. What irked me more was that this lady was a Vice President. I was amazed at the bank's doggedness that they had sent a VP to solicit business!

> *A wise man would not speak unless he had listened. A wise man would talk less and hear more. A wise man would not jump to conclusions. A wise man would avoid putting his foot in his mouth.*

I was about to send her away when I suddenly decided to take out my pent-up anger on her. I asked her to be sent in and even without offering her a seat started off. I vented out all my spleen and the poor young lady swallowed all my insults. Once I finished, she started slowly.

She was the Secretary of a woman's club and they had decided to honour me for my contribution to the society. At that moment I wished that the earth would split open and swallow me.

Be extremely wary of tall claims

A survivor must be extremely wary of tall claims of any type, such as:

1. Rock bottom prices
2. Too much of a discount
3. Too heavy an advertisement
4. Newspaper or media advertisement selling any medicine or medical treatment
5. Stock clearance sales with more than 50% discount
6. Cut price buffet meals in a five star hotel (In this case, it is indeed a weekly stock clearance of the leftovers from the deep freezer)
7. Organisations offering you awards. You only have to advertise in their souvenir
8. A free credit card
9. A credit card company that promises to absorb all your old credits
10. A dog that doesn't bark or barks too much
11. The pizza shop that gives you one pizza free for every pizza purchased
12. Your alma mater inviting you as a chief guest
13. A hundred and seventy-five rupees a kilo detergent suddenly slashed to fifty rupees a kilo.

> *A survivor does not fall for tall claims. There is no such thing as a free ticket. Nor is there anything called a real bargain. There are always hidden strings attached if a thing is really too good.*

PEARL 14 — Not all things in life can be bargained

The grandfather was a little reluctant to send his grandson for shopping because the boy was a simpleton. The old man was worried that the boy would be cheated. He asked the young lad not to purchase anything without bargaining. The boy lacked extensive vocabulary and did not know what 'Bargaining' meant.

"To offer to pay fifty rupees for a product that costs a hundred is called bargaining," explained the grandfather. He then handed some money to the boy and asked him to buy an umbrella.

> *Survivors thus know that there are times when you bargain while there are situations where you know that the price tag shows only one price which is a fixed price.*

The boy got to the shop and enquired about the cost of a good umbrella. The shopkeeper showed him a product and told him that it cost a hundred rupees. "I shall pay you fifty," chirped the lad.

The shopkeeper was shocked because no one had bargained so dramatically in his shop. He did some calculations. His purchase price was rupees sixty. He was carrying a dead stock for a long time and decided to liquidate it. He smiled at the boy and said "OK, take it."

The boy gave a smile and said, "I will pay you twenty-five!"

The shopkeeper was irritated and shouted, "You are the limit. Here, take it for free!"

"OK. Give me two!"

PEARL 15 — Be wary of self-styled consultants

The professor had a tomcat who was an absolute Casanova. He used to be away all night and indulge in fights over the female cats of the locality. He used to get back home in the early hours of the morning, torn and tatty. Finally, the professor could take it no more and consulted the veterinary who advised that the animal should be gelded. The professor agreed and the tomcat was surgically castrated. Six months later, the vet met the professor and asked him about the cat's nocturnal habits. With a sigh the professor said, "Oh, he still stays out all night but now he has become a consultant!"

> *So the next time someone advises you to hire an outside consultant to tell you how to do your work, be extremely wary.*

Remember, a consultant has really nothing to lose–he actually gambles on your money. Have you ever asked him that if he knew all the things that should be done the right way which would make you rich and famous, then why did he not use them himself and become a millionaire instead of selling his talents and time for a few thousands?

I never have nor ever will employ a consultant. And most wise men would do the same. Is it not rightly said that advice is the easiest thing to give?

16 Intelligent enemy vs stupid friend

This is a story from Panchatantra tales, which is a chronicle full of lovely stories with excellent morals.

A dense jungle lay between two kingdoms. A cruel bandit occupied the jungle and used to waylay the people who crossed it and snatch away all their possessions. Three jewellers had to carry a large ruby each from one place to another and camped at the edge of the forest. A thief who was observing them befriended them. The thief cautioned them about the bandit. He told them that he too was a jeweller and was carrying a ruby across. He then told them that to avoid detection, he had swallowed his ruby. Based on his advice the other three jewellers did the same and decided to travel together. The thief had planned to mix poison in their food in the night and later slit their stomach to extract the rubies.

> Survivors avoid fools like the plague. To have a fool as a friend, servant, subordinate or spouse is courting disaster. A stupid friend has the potential to cause a lot more damage than an intelligent enemy.

To their misfortune, the bandit gang waylaid them on the way and took them to their boss. The bandit boss had a parrot that could look at the travellers and tell if they had hidden anything on their body. On seeing the four travellers (the three jewellers and the thief), the parrot started screaming out aloud that they had something hidden on their bodies. A thorough search did not produce anything. The boss then insinuated that they had swallowed the valuables, which the four travellers hotly denied. It was apparent that their bellies would be slit open one by one to find out the hidden jewels. The thief was an intelligent fellow and realised that if the jewellers had their bellies slit and the rubies found, he too would not escape and his protests would fall on deaf ears.

However, if he offered to sacrifice himself, the bandit would find no valuables in his belly. The jewellers would thus be saved. He had to die in either case but if he chooses the second option, at least three lives would be saved.

He was killed and his belly did not yield any valuables. In a fit of anger the bandit killed his parrot. The other three jewellers however escaped unhurt.

The corollary of this parable is given below:-

The prince had a pet monkey who was devout and obedient. But being a monkey he was devoid of intelligence. Once the Queen Mother was sleeping and the prince instructed the monkey to fan her while he went for a hunt. After some time a fly started buzzing over the face of the queen and would not go away despite vigorous fanning. The agitated monkey picked up a huge granite boulder and smashed the fly. He crushed the queen's head too!

In the first story, the thief was an enemy but helpful, while in the second story, the monkey was a stupid friend.

PEARL 17 — One who changes with change survives

One of the best selling management books is called "Who— moved —my—Cheese?" It is a million-copy best-seller in which a philosophy is discussed in the form of a parable. It goes like this:

Three mice lived in a maze with a complex array of rooms, each full of delicious cheese. The place had numerous rooms and myriads of pathways. Each room was chock-a-block with cheese and the three mice spent a lot of time chewing the cheese. With no problems it was a trio of happy and content mice indeed.

> *A survivor must expect change. He must anticipate changing situations and change himself to adapt to the change.*

One fine day when the mice woke up, they found that the first few rooms were totally empty. Somehow, mysteriously all the cheese had disappeared. The first mouse moaned and cursed and stayed in place, starving and hungry. The other two mice set about exploring the complex mazes and the intricate pathways in search of more cheese. It was indeed a complex maze and one of the two kept cribbing and commenting about the additional trouble that had been thrust on them. But the other mice continued on relentlessly. After some time they reached another section which was stocked with cheese but this was neither as abundant nor as fresh as the cheese in the first room.

One mouse ate a bit of the rancid cheese and was aghast. He muttered "It is better to starve than to eat such stale food." He got back to the first room and starved with his other colleague. The third mouse however was not the one to accept defeat so easily. He continued undeterred onward and continued to survive on the stale cheese. The taste was horrid and the smell awful. He almost felt like vomiting but still continued chomping and chewing his way through the maze.

The two hungry and weak mice left behind now realised that they would not survive if they did not eat. One mouse proclaimed that something was better than nothing and that they could at least survive on rotten and rancid cheese rather than perish due to starvation. They set out again but by now it was too late. Their bodies were very weak and they could not progress further. Half way down the maze they died of starvation.

The third mouse however had gone way ahead. The cheese too had started tasting better. It was not that the rancid cheese was suddenly replaced by fresh cheese. It was just that he had got used to the cheese and his body had already adapted to it. He went on undeterred and at the end of the maze found out fresh stocks of abundant cheese. Fresh and tasty. The third mouse thus remained happy, satiated and alive.

Do compete but in a healthy way

A king had two sons. The younger one was jealous of his elder brother. He was upset whenever the king gave his elder son something. The king was a little worried about his son's attitude. One day, he summoned his younger son and told him that he was willing to give him anything that he asked: money, gold, riches, kingdom, whatever. The younger son could ask anything within reason and the wish would be fulfilled. The young prince was pleased, but then his father set a condition. He told the younger prince that the elder prince would be given double of whatever the younger one received. The younger prince told his father that he needed a day to think and make up his mind. He came back the next day and told his father: "Please take this big needle and poke it in my right eye." The young prince did not mind losing one eye for the pleasure of seeing his brother go blind.

> *We should be competitive in a positive way and not by pulling down others.*

The competitiveness in our present context is such that the real goal gets lost in the maze of competition. Eventually, an attitude develops where a person is happier to see his colleague failing than he himself succeeding. Instead of improving one's own performance, a person spends all his time pulling down others.

It is correctly said that a basket of crabs needs no lid. Just as one crab climbs up to the edge, the other will pull it down. "So what if I cannot escape? So long as I ensure that he too does not, I am happy."

Pearl 19: Never underestimate the capabilities of others

This had happened many many years ago when I was on a train journey with my wife. We had purchased first class tickets and as with other newly married couples would have appreciated some privacy. But we had an additional occupant in our compartment who was a bearded Swami who looked extremely shabby. He spoke in chaste Tamil and we conversed with him in this language. However, when my wife and I had to discuss confidential issues we would switch over to English. After a short while we grew bold and started criticising him and passing sarcastic comments in English, certain that he did not know the language. He travelled in our compartment for the next eight hours and all along, while we were polite to him when we spoke to him in Tamil, we really teased him and made fun of him while we conversed amongst ourselves in English. Just as he got down at his destination, he gifted us something wrapped in brown paper. Only after the train started again did I open the wrapping. It was a book in English discussing Shiva worship in Dravidian cultures. The last page showed a photograph of the author who was none else but our co-passenger. And it was modestly mentioned that the author was an M.A. in English Literature from Oxford University in England.

> *A survivor should never take things for granted. He should never underestimate the capabilities of the others.*

The embarrassment felt by the British Airways pilot would have paled before that felt by my wife and me. The book still finds a place of pride on my bookshelf and each time I look at it, I learn the lesson once again.

PEARL 20: Avoid stubborn people, don't try to change them

A king was once travelling in his lavishly decorated chariot when he saw a beggar on the street. He tossed a copper coin to the beggar who missed it. The coin rolled past him and fell into a sewer. Undeterred, the beggar plunged his hand into the filth and tried to extricate the coin. The king wrinkled his nose in disgust and called the beggar close. He threw another coin. The beggar put this coin into his pocket and walked back to the sewer to search the other one.

> *Some people never change. They are so rigid in their attitudes that they would perish and yet remain obsessed with their one-track mind and attitude. Survivors don't waste time and effort over them. Avoid them or bypass them.*

The king was intrigued by the beggar's greed and tossed him a silver coin. The beggar collected it and walked back to the drain. The king threw a gold coin, and the same thing happened again. He kept giving costlier gifts each time and once the beggar collected it, he went back to the drain.

Finally, the king called him close and told him that he was willing to give him half his kingdom. The beggar said that he wanted **that** half of the kingdom through which **that** particular drain flowed!

PEARL 21 — If it is too good, there has to be a catch in it

A millionaire was entering J.F.K Airport when he saw a yuppie walking with two heavy suitcases, one in each hand. The millionaire asked the yuppie for the time. Placing the two heavy boxes on the floor, he unrolled his sleeve and displayed his watch. It was a unique instrument with a fancy dial. He checked up and told the time in eleven world capitals. He then pressed a button and the millionaire could see a television broadcast with the newscaster reading out the latest news. He then pressed a button and made a phone call to his wife. Finally, he pointed the watch to the millionaire and took his photos with the very same watch! The millionaire was impressed. All that jazz in just one wrist watch! He wanted the watch. His wife would be impressed. He wanted to buy it but the yuppie was reluctant to sell. Hard bargaining followed and finally a deal was struck for a hundred thousand dollars. The millionaire snapped the watch around his wrist and was about to walk away when the yuppie stopped him. He pointed towards the two heavy boxes and said, "Sir, you are forgetting the batteries!"

> *We should not plunge into any deal unless we are absolutely sure as to what we are getting for our money. Any scheme that looks too good to be true is certainly too good to be true.*

Non-apparent or hidden liabilities are something that we should be wary of.

PEARL 22
Have faith, it helps

A Christian pastor, a hippie, a millionaire and the world's most intelligent man were flying in a small plane when the engines started failing one by one. It was apparent that the plane would crash and the only option was to strap on the parachutes and jump. But there was a small problem. There were only four parachutes and the pilot said that he would be using one. He left it to his passengers to decide as to who would remain without a parachute.

Before they could start discussing the problem, the intelligent man said, "I don't know about you three, but I am too precious to die." Strapping on a parachute he jumped out leaving three co-passengers shocked. The rich man looked at the pastor and asked: "Now, what do we do, Father?" The priest smiled and replied: "Originally, I had decided that the three of you could have a parachute each and I would pray to God for guidance. And look, God has shown us the way. The most intelligent man has jumped down with the hippie's backpack!"

> *Faith does move mountains. It gives us a point or goal to fix. It gives us something to look for support. It gives us a purpose in life. It gives us some order amidst chaos.*

Corruption and bribes

Corruption is something that has seeped into the very fibre of our being. At least in India, corruption has become an inseparable part of our day to day lives. An exporter I met recently told me that his bribe overheads was twenty to twenty-five percent of his turnover. Yes! It is not a printing mistake. It is a quarter of his turnover and not a quarter of his profits!

But then corruption is not a new phenomenon. It is as old as mankind itself and this is again a parable from our ancient times.

The king had to employ his wife's brother in his organisation. This fellow was sly and crooked, and soon earned a reputation of being corrupt. Extremely corrupt rather. At the treasury where he fiddled with the accounts. He was posted to the granary where he sold grains at a premium. When put in charge of mines he stole gold, when in charge of the fields or farm, he stole grain or poultry. Being the king's brother-in-law, he could not be sacked. The king grew vexed and finally decided to give him a job where he could not get bribes. He was given his new job as a counter of waves. Yes. His job was to sit on the seashore and count the waves!

> *Take corruption like eczema. It is not going to kill you. Treat it as far as you can. But if you keep on raising your blood pressure over it all the time, the blood pressure is going to kill you!*

The king was sure that at least in this way he would not be able to collect bribes. A few days later, a minister sent to check up on him got the shock of his life. The brother-in-law was sitting on the beach and the fisher folk came to him one by one and gave him a silver coin each. This they had to give him to be allowed to launch their fishing boats because as an official 'Wave-Counter', the king's brother-in-law told them that they were disturbing the waves and spoiling his calculation!

One who grabs the opportunities shall survive

Once, a pastor's village was assailed by floods. His neighbours started vacating the village. When they asked him also to move, he refused saying that his faith and God would protect him. The water rose and the whole village was submerged. A swimmer swam by and stopped at the pastor's place. He had strong arms and offered to carry the pastor on his back as he swam. The pastor refused. A little later, a rescue boat appeared. The pastor refused to budge. Finally, a helicopter appeared and dropped down a ladder. The priest still refused. Eventually, the flood swallowed his house and he died. Being a good man of faith, he went straight to heaven. The moment he landed he complained to God that despite his faith, God did not save him. "Oh, but I sent you a swimmer, a boat and even a chopper! You never utilised an opportunity!" said God, with a smile. The stubborn priest had missed all the opportunities that were presented to him.

> *You never know in which form an opportunity would knock on your door. A survivor should always be prepared to recognise it and grab it!*

In our lives, we find a lot of opportunities. If we don't seize them with both hands, it is our own fault. And it is for this that we need preparedness. We must be prepared to grab the opportunity when it comes.

Be kind to others, it helps you too

Acharya Vinobha Bhave was a simple man and would usually remain barefoot. One of the industrialists, who was his patron, got him a fancy pair of soft chappals from England. He had taken special care to get it made of synthetic material because the Acharya would not wear footwear made of leather. Once, the Acharya had to travel by train and reached the platform just as the train had started off. In the melee of getting in, one slipper fell down between the tracks. Before the train picked up speed, he threw the other one too! "Who ever finds the slippers, let him find a pair so that it would be useful for him!"

Most often, we are so busy looking after our own selfish needs that we forget altruism totally. Donations for claiming income tax benefits is not altruism. Film stars spending an hour in the school for the mentally retarded is not altruism because all they want is a coverage in the press the following day.

The mere fact that you make up your mind and develop a genuine desire to reach out to others will do you a world of good.

Genuine and unselfish help is the one that is done without expecting a reward. Do it and you will be pleased at the inner satisfaction it gives you. You need not always spend money to help others.

The wonders of mutual help

Once Lord Vishnu, the Supreme God invited both, the Devas and the Asuras for dinner. But He wanted to test their intelligence and talent. Hence, before being allowed to enter the dining hall, each guest had a stick tied between his arm and forearm, making his elbow rigid and unbending. Obviously, a straight elbow would not reach the mouth and Lord Vishnu wanted to see how the two groups tackled the situation. He first visited the room with the Asuras and found absolute chaos and confusion with no one able to eat properly. When He went to the room of the Devas, it was all peace and quiet with the Devas seated in a big circle, and each person feeding the man across him! And that's the big difference between the Devas and the Asuras.

A society of Asura-like selfish people would end up hungry and frustrated while a mutually helpful society of Deva-like people would prosper!

We don't always do things that benefit just us. It can benefit someone else too. If we do good for someone, then someone else would do good for us. A divisive society in which each member tries to do things only for himself or herself is doomed to crabs and decadence. A cohesive society where each of us unselfishly assists his peer would be vibrant, orderly and progressive.

PEARL 27
Reign in your jealousy, man

A famous psychiatrist in Paris once had a very depressed patient. The good doctor tried all his therapeutic techniques without any success. The young man before him was in such great throes of melancholy and depression that nothing the psychiatrist did helped him. Finally the doctor said, "A new circus is playing in the town. It is said that Ronaldo the clown has an act in the circus. His jokes are so funny and antics so humorous that no one can resist laughing. I advise you to go to the circus and spend some time. I am sure that all your depression would go away." The young man stood up with dejection on his face and said, "But Sir, I am Ronaldo the clown!" When you see a multi-millionaire travelling in his chauffer-driven Mercedes, you give out a sigh of jealousy because you think that he is the happiest man in the world. For all you know, his wife could be cheating on him, his son might have become a drug addict, his daughter might have eloped with a low-class man and the man himself must be facing an income tax case!

> *Life is much bigger than the trappings of life. Before you feel jealous about someone, you must realise that you don't really know how that man himself feels about his life!*

Just because someone appears affluent does not mean that he is really happy with life.

PEARL 28 — When in trouble, don't seek the easy way out

Alzheimer's disease is a condition in which the brain tissue degenerates. The most common symptom of this disease is total forgetfulness. You, of course, know all about AIDS. Mr. Sharma received a call from the hospital about Mrs. Sharma's blood tests. It seemed that another Mrs. Sharma had also given her blood for test and some mix up had taken place. The other Mrs. Sharma had gone away and the hospital could not call her back for another test. They wondered if Mr. Sharma could get his wife along for another blood test. Mr. Sharma was visibly upset at this goof-up and told the hospital that his wife too could not come for a repeat blood test. "Anyway, what do the tests show?" "Well, Sir, one Mrs. Sharma is suffering from Alzheimer's disease and one from AIDS." "What do I do now?" "Simple, Sir. Drop your wife at the *kumbh mela*. If she comes back to your house, don't sleep with her!"

> When faced with two equally difficult choices, the easier one is most likely to be the wrong choice. Life does not prefer short-cuts. One must think twice before taking an easy way out of any situation because the long term consequences could be far-reaching and disastrous. On many occasions, we don't get a second chance to allow us to learn from our mistakes.

That's a joke but all of us face an occasion some time or the other in our lives when the two choices before us are equally difficult.

PEARL 29: An idiot can mess up everything—avoid him

During the Second World War, the Allied army introduced new hand grenades. While the earlier ones would explode exactly four seconds after the pin was pulled, the second generation grenades had an eight-second timer. These grenades met with universal approval except with the Polish regiment. The Polish soldiers suffered from a strange sort of injuries. Instead of having blasted thumbs and palms, they had blasted testicles. No good reason for this could be found.

They decided to conduct an enquiry for which a Polish sergeant was invited. They asked him how he trained his men to use the grenades. His reply was correct. Pull the pin, count to seven and hurl it at the enemy. Everything seemed to be correct. The British were puzzled even more. Finally, the Polish sergeant was handed over a dummy grenade and asked to demonstrate as to how he taught his men to use it. He picked up the grenade in his right hand and took it to his mouth. He yanked the pin with his teeth. He then started counting the fingers of his left hand–one–two–three–four–and–five. He then grasped the grenade between his legs and continued to count–six and–seven on the other hand!

> *You can devise the most sophisticated instrument and incorporate all the fail-safe devices, but you cannot actually make it "idiot-safe". Survivors learn to avoid keeping company of fools.*

PEARL 30 — You better accept Murphy's Law

A restaurant is New York boasted of a thousand dishes, right from monkey brain fry to lizard stew, fried bats' wings, roast rabbits, possum curry, parrot soup and tortoise grilled. You name it and you could order it. A Japanese tourist stared at the menu card for a long time and finally settled on an elephant tail sandwich. A few moments later, a distraught waiter came back with the message that the order could not be filled. Due to a bakers' strike in New York, they had run out of bread slices! This story is Murphy's Law personified.

> Well, these things do happen and will happen. There is no need to get worked up on them.

When something has to go wrong, even the most trivial reason is enough. Extremely small errors have resulted in calamitous conclusions. Anything that can go wrong will go wrong for reasons anticipated as well as unexpected. It always rains on the day we forget the umbrella.

The best movie comes on your favourite channel when you have already booked your tickets for the opera. The scrawny old man who you mistake for a gardener in your latest girlfriend's house turns out to be her father. And when you spend hard earned money on a book on art of living, you get something like this!

Pearl 31: Beware of all that looks too good

When you are made an offer which appears to be unrealistically attractive, in all probability it is just that—unrealistic! Take the scheme of time share holidays where you pay today but start enjoying it twenty-five years later! Or take a second hand car salesman who tries to sell you an immaculate single owner lady doctor driven car at a low price. He only forgets to tell you that it was almost smashed flat in a pileup! Or the envelopes that come by post with scratch away numbers. If the digits match, you get a prize. The only problem is that the sender is in Germany and you have to send ten dollars as handling charges to get your winnings cheque. Or schemes in which they would plant teak trees for you so that in a hundred years, your grandchildren can reap the riches. Survivors must learn to curb the natural desire of short-cuts. You cannot get selected in IIT by studying ten important questions. You cannot get rich by some secret business technique—in all probability it will be a fraud and land you in jail.

> There are no short-cuts to success or riches or whatever. Everything comes only after the effort which is due to it has been spent on it. If someone claims the contrary, rest assured there is a hidden catch in it.

Learning to cope with the pressure around you demands will-power. People will tempt you, they will even quote examples that so-and-so made so much money in such a short time. You must resist them.

Pearl 32: Keep expectations high, but not too high

A poor Brahmin was accursed by poverty. He wanted riches. He decided to do penance, prayers and austerities to God. He went to the Himalayas and did penance for thirty-six years before God appeared in his presence. The moment he saw God, the anxious Brahmin said:

> *I am not saying that one should not be ambitious or aim high. By all means, do it and give it your best shot. Still, if you don't get it, thank God for His mercies and be happy with whatever you get.*

"Oh Lord! I have been performing prayers and austerities for thirty-six long years. What took you so long?"

God gave a benevolent smile and said:

"Time varies greatly on the cosmic side. Your time passes very quickly while ours passes slowly. To you, it might have been thirty-six years but as far as I am concerned it has only taken me a fraction of a second since you thought about me!"

The Brahmin asked, "And so God, is money too variable on the cosmic scale?"

God answered: "Yes indeed. A single gold coin would buy anything on your earth."

The Brahmin had greed in his eyes as he said, "Then God, I would request you to give me a coin."

God nodded and said, "Just a minute. I will get it."

And disappeared!

Genies are for kids and not for you

Adam Smith was one of the happiest men on earth. At twenty-six, he had graduated Summa Cum Laude from Oxford University, inherited a million pounds from his grandfather's estate and got engaged to the prettiest twenty-two-year old girl in London. At that moment, Adam Smith's only regret was his golf handicap. He wanted to score a scratch on the eleventh hole at least once before he got married and thus took his fiancée to the golf course on a Sunday afternoon.

A chance shot diverted the ball to a cottage beyond the golf course and the ball crashed a window as it entered in. Rules of golf say that a ball has to be played from where it has fallen and thus Adam Smith and his fiancée walked hesitantly to the hut. They gently pushed the door and entered the cottage where they found a bearded and turbaned Swami sitting in meditation. The saint looked up to the diffident couple and explained with a smile that he was a genie who had been just released from a bottle shattered by a golf ball. He was so pleased that he was willing to grant Adam Smith three wishes.

> *Survivors refuse to be taken in for a ride by clever sales gimmicks. The next time a salesman promises you the moon and stars, ask him if he has a space suit!*

The young man was ecstatic and did not take too long to blurt out his wish list. He wanted his one million pound stocks to escalate to ten. He wanted the most lavish wedding in London. And he wanted to score one better than the club golf pro! The genie seemed to consider the wishes for some time and then said:

"I can fulfil all your wishes. But having stayed cooped up inside a bottle for so long has made me long for female companionship.

Thus, in exchange for the three wishes, I want you to leave your fiancée with me for the night." It was a Hobson's choice, but then the rewards were so tempting that Mr. Adam Smith took the easy way out. It needed less than ten minutes to convince the fiancée and Mr. Smith left the two in the cottage and walked out with a heavy heart. But then he consoled himself that the rewards that he was getting were tremendous!

The next morning he saw his fiancée draped only in a towel, sitting snugly on the genie's lap. She came to him with some reluctance.

"Now for my wishes!" said Adam Smith.

"Can I ask you a question?" said the genie.

"Oh, go ahead!" said Adam Smith.

"How old are you?" asked the genie.

"I am twenty-six!" replied Adam Smith.

"Aren't you a little too old to believe in bottles and genies?" retorted the genie.

34. It is childish to act on impulse

To be human is to be born impulsive. We simply cannot help remaining impulsive because we are born that way. The impulsiveness of putting a finger into the fire, or plucking a bee's wings or touching a bench marked with a "Wet Paint" board are all decisions which are reflexive actions. Only as we grow up do we mature and learn to curb and curtail these actions.

But in times of crises, we often forget the cardinal rule of 'think before you leap'. The fact that between ready and fire, we have to <u>aim</u> is overlooked. We squeeze the trigger even before ensuring if the sights are lined to the correct target. This is well illustrated by the next anecdote.

A man called up his house from Dubai and the phone call was received by the maid. The conversation went as follows:

Master: Please summon Madam.

Maid: I am sorry Sir, Mistress is not to be disturbed.

> *Any decision taken on an impulse without considering its consequences would undoubtedly boomerang on us.*

Master: Hey, hey! Don't you realise that I am her husband? Call her to the phone immediately.

Maid: But Sir! I am sorry Sir!

Master: Now, now! Don't panic. Listen to me carefully and answer all my questions correctly.

Maid: Yes Master.

Master: Is the Madam in the house?

Maid: Yes, Sir.

Master: Where is she?

Maid: In the bedroom.

Master: Is she alone?

Maid: No.

Master: Is the bedroom locked.

Maid: Yes, Master. It is bolted from inside.

Master: Who is with her?

Maid: Sir, Master, ... Hmm...., Sir!

Master: Please don't panic. I am the master. Please tell me, who is in the bedroom?

Maid: It is the young Abdullah from the neighbourhood.

Master: Now listen to me carefully and do exactly as I say. Walk to the study and pull out my pistol from the cupboard. Go straight and knock on the bedroom. When the door opens, shoot my wife and her lover in their hearts. Do you understand?

Maid: Yes, Master. I will do it.

The phone was placed beside the cradle and five minutes later, the master could hear two gunshots. The maid came back to the phone.

Master: Have you done it?

Maid: Yes, Master. Both are dead.

Master: That is good. Now go straight to the swimming pool in the rear and toss the pistol into it.

Maid: Swimming pool?

Master: Yes, the swimming pool in the rear garden.

Maid: But Sir, our house doesn't have a swimming pool.

Master: What? Is it not 664231692?

PEARL 35: Don't fall into the trap of 'if he can do it, so can I'

The view from the top of the Empire State Building was spectacular. That day, a white fluffy cloud floated about ten feet below the roof top and a dozen awestruck tourists admired the scene. One tourist was explaining to the Japanese next to him, "The upper surfaces of the clouds have so much surface tension that if you jump from here, the cloud would bounce you back to the roof top." The Japanese tourist gave a disbelieving laugh as he lisped, "No believe American. American tell lies!" The American stood on the ledge and jumped down. Exactly as he had claimed, the cloud bounced him like a gigantic pillow and landed him softly back on the top floor. The Japanese tourist was stupefied but was still not convinced. The American repeated his trick once again with identical results. The Japanese tourist had a big smile as he un-slung his camera, binoculars and video camera which he handed to the American. He perched himself on the edge and took a dive. Penetrating the cloud, he fell straight down 102 storeys onto the pavement and died instantly. The pretty girl standing next to the American tourist said softy, "*That was a nasty trick you played, Superman!*"

This happens in all walks of life. Just because someone else does something or is capable of doing something, it is neither a pointer nor an order for you also to try that. You have to decide for yourself what is good or desirable for you. If someone made good money out of a chemist's shop does not mean that you can also make money by that. Maybe the locality where he operated suited a chemist's shop; maybe your locality is not close to any hospital, therefore a chemist's shop may not do good business.

> *What is sauce for the goose is not necessarily sauce for the gander.*

Tangential thinking profitable thinking

Orthopaedic surgery employs a lot of drilling, boring, burring and tapping tools. I purchased one from a Swiss company and paid about thirty-five thousand rupees in those times. After about a year's use, I found that it had a mechanical problem. The local dealer told me that it had to be sent to Singapore for repairs, which would take about six weeks. Too impatient to wait, I decided to look into the matter myself. I took the drill to a machine shop. Initially, I was hesitant in dismantling such a costly product but decided to take the plunge. Once it was opened up fully, the problem became apparent. A vane in it called Hylum vane had snapped. It took just about half an hour to fabricate it and cost me practically nothing. While it was being fixed, the machinist looked at the other components. He told me that it looked similar to the industrial pneumatic drill except for the fact that it had no rusting parts. All surgical instruments need to be steam sterilised before surgical operations. Everything that was made of iron in an industrial drill had been replaced. The body was thus made of phosphor bronze, the gears of stainless steel and the ball bearings of chrome cobalt. In less than two weeks, the machinist and I could buy an industrial drill and change its rusting parts to make a copy that cost just about two thousand rupees! I opened a small unit to produce more of them for Indian surgeons and in three years' time it grew into a four-and-a-half crore medical instruments manufacturing unit!

> *Keep your eyes and ears open, and your antenna extended. A little tangential thinking is sure to provide us with profitable solutions to unexpected problems.*

If you are learning something from somebody, learn it fully

The mice were worried by the problem that was the cat. They could not even come out of their holes because the cat would pounce on them. The worried mice convened a meeting and decided to hire a consultant. The consultant advised that they should tie a bell around the cat's neck so that they would be alerted by its arrival and could scamper away to safety. The consultant was about to collect the money and walk away when a little mouse asked: "But who will bell the cat?" The consultant tucked the money in his pocket and said, "That is for you to find out!" Once he had gone away, the rats sat together again to decide as to how to bell the cat. The little mouse suggested that they should approach the dog. "Please tie this bell around the cat's neck. We will pay you an appropriate fee," the rats requested the dog. "But why do you want to bell the cat?" asked the curious dog. "You don't need to ask this question," said the mice, handing over the money and the bell. The dog agreed, collected the fee and the bell. The next day the bell was around the cat's neck. The rats were all happy, but got the greatest shock of their lives when the cat pounced and caught hold of one of them. They realised with horror that the cat did have a bell around its neck but it did not tinkle. It was a silent bell with its gong bead missing. They rushed to the dog to complain. The dog looked up lazily and said, "Yes, I removed the gong bead because my little one wanted to play with it. You only asked me to tie the bell. You never told me that it had to be a bell that rang!"

> *If you are learning something from somebody, learn it completely. If you are hiring somebody to do something, ensure that he does it fully and does not withhold something crucial.*

PEARL 38 — Savour the love of your loved ones before it is too late

A busy life had resulted in a situation in which I was not able to spend much time with my family. I returned home late and would find my six-year-old daughter already asleep. I would have one drink too many in the night and sleep till late. By the time I woke up next day, my daughter would be gone to school. Sundays were spent in pursuing hobbies.

One Sunday I was going out with my friends when my daughter rushed towards me. She was upset that I was leaving her again and was not taking her along. She told me that she was making a special gift for me which would be ready only by the afternoon. She wanted me to return soon so that I could un-wrap it in her presence. But I was held up with my buddies and by the time I came back, it was almost two in the night and my daughter was fast asleep. Nevertheless I saw a small box packed with craft paper in a way only a six-year-old could do. I lifted the box and it was light. I shook it from side to side but no sound came. I hastily un-wrapped the box and found that it was empty. I was a little puzzled and tossed it aside. The next morning I was woken up early by my daughter who was all ready to go to school. She asked me with a flush of excitement if I had got her gift. I told her that it was an empty box. "But Daddy, I had filled it with a hundred kisses for you!" she said a little sadly. I had become so involved in my pursuit of pleasures that I had not been able to recognise her hundred kisses.

We are all stuck in the race of success or pleasures and don't have time for our loved ones. By the time we realise it, it is too late.

> The love of your loved ones that you miss today or ignore today will never come back.

Pearl 39: The importance of proper data evaluation

A cop caught four unruly youth on Marina Beach. The cop house had a new lie detector machine and the four of them were taken to the police station. The first man was connected to the machine and asked:

"What were you doing on the beach? What was the fight and commotion all about?"

With a straight face he said:

"Oh it was nothing. I was just throwing peanut into the sea!"

The machine indicated that he was not lying and he was released.

The second and third man too answered identically:

"We were just throwing peanut into the sea!"

In management terms the following aphorism says it all: If you don't evaluate the available data properly, you are liable to draw erroneous conclusions.

Having released the three innocent people, the cop glowered at the fourth.

He hissed as he proceeded to strap the lie detector machine on.

"And so it is you who is the real culprit, is it?"

The fourth man said softly, "I don't know about being a culprit but my name sure is Peanut!"

PEARL 40
Talent always costs money

*O*nce Emperor Akbar was surrounded by his courtiers. His Chief Minister Birbal had not yet arrived. The other courtiers were jealous that Birbal got a salary many times theirs. In his absence they started questioning the king about this discrepancy. Just then loud music and noises of a wedding procession became audible. The king asked a courtier:

"Find out who the bride is!" The courtier returned in a few minutes with the requisite information. The king then asked the second courtier: "Who is the groom?" He too left and came back with the information. In this manner the king asked about the bride's father's name, the groom's father's name and other details. Each time another courtier would go and fetch appropriate information.

> *A talent pool costs money but is cheaper in the long run. In an organisation it is best to hire the best you can afford. And the better the talent, the more expensive would it be.*

While the last chap had come back with the groom's father's name, they all grew silent because they saw Birbal coming. After greetings were exchanged the king said: "Well Birbal! I hear some sounds. It appears as if a wedding procession is outside. Please find out the bride's father's name!"

Birbal nodded and walked out. He came back in ten minutes and said: "Oh Emperor! So and so, son of so and so from such and such village is marrying this girl from this village." He continued to tell all the details and ended with the menu list for the wedding. Akbar looked at his courtiers and said: "Now you know why I pay Birbal as much as I do!"

A management axiom clearly says it all: "Throw peanuts and you would get only monkeys. If you want intelligent and capable employees, you need to pay real money!"

PEARL 41
Do not follow blindly

A novice monk was walking by the riverbank when he saw three monks sitting and meditating. He, too, sat beside them, closed his eyes and started his meditations. A little later, the first monk got up and walked to the river. He folded his hands in prayer before the river and walked on the water. He walked across to the other side and after a short while, walked back the same way. A little later, the second and then the third monk did the same. The apprentice monk was impressed. He, too, walked to the flowing river and folded his hands in prayer. He too attempted to walk across the river but was washed away. The three monks looked at each other and murmured softly, "Maybe we should have told him the location of the submerged stepping stones!"

> *Deep down in our hearts, we know as to what we are capable of doing and what we are not. Thoughtless aping of others might drown us like the apprentice monk.*

Not everyone is capable of doing everything.

What not to forget

A man and his wife had invited their friends for dinner. The husbands were in the lounge sipping beer while the wives were in the kitchen, heating the food and arranging the dishes. One of the guys started describing a Mexican restaurant that he had visited the previous week. The host blurted out, "My wife and I too went to a Thai restaurant last week. The food was really good!" "What was the name of the restaurant?" asked the other friend. The host furrowed his forehead but was not able to recall. He thought and thought. He then said, "What is that flower?" "Rose?" asked a friend. "Nope! The one that grows in ponds!" said the host. "You mean a lotus?" asked the other friend. "No, no. Not the lotus. It is white in colour," said the host. The others got it. "A lily," they shouted in a chorus. The host's face lit with a big smile. Turning to the kitchen he shouted, "Lily! Lily darling! What was the restaurant we went to last week? That Japanese or Thai place?"

> There are things in life you must never forget. If you are a married man, this includes your wife's birthday and your marriage anniversary. If your in-laws are alive, don't forget to ring them up on their marriage aniversary. Saves you a lot of trouble.

Memory is a strange thing. Though each human brain is anatomically identical to any other individual human brain, there is a remarkable difference from one to the other. People vary widely in their capacity to remember. Scientists define memory as short term and long term. Short term memory is said to be related to electrical charges in the human brain and is relatively temporary. It is like a charge of a cell phone battery. Most of our routine day-to-day activities form this sort of a memory. Long term memory, on the other hand, seems to be more complex and is probably stored as a chemical and biological response at a cellular level.

Pearl 43

Rules for alcohol

It is true that an alcoholic would always find an excuse for his drinking habit. Alcohol is a good thing. Alcoholics and reckless drinkers have spoiled its name. The British Medical Association has given fourteen units a week rule. A unit would be a glass of beer, or half a glass of wine or thirty millilitres of hard liquor. Anything more and it affects us in many ways. Alcohol makes the drinker loquacious and an irritant. He loses control of his tongue. It has not spared even great people like George Bernard Shaw, as this anecdote would illustrate.

> *Dilution-Duration-Diet-Density-Sun Down.*

Once George Bernard Shaw was seated next to a socialite at a dinner. Shaw was a little inebriated and his speech was slurred and words a little vulgar. The lady next to him could not take too much of it and said haughtily, "Mr. Shaw! You are drunk!"

With a characteristic drawl, Shaw replied,

"Madam! I am drunk and you are ugly! At least I would wake up a sober man tomorrow!"

If you have to drink, you had better follow the English tradition of the five D's. **Dilution** means only wines or beers. If spirits are consumed, they should be appropriately diluted. **Duration** indicates the period over which the alcohol is consumed. It is foolish to gulp down one drink after the other. Slow and steady is the name of the game. **Diet** is what you munch when you drink. Cheese or pizza would coat the inside of your stomach and delay the absorption of alcohol. **Density** is actually a synonym for quantity. Drink in moderation. **Sun Down** indicates another rule. Never drink before sunset. This helps us in more ways than one. You are less likely to go out of your house in the nights. Even if you become tipsy, at least you will not pick up a fight with a stranger!

PEARL 44 — There is no use gilding the lily

An industrialist decided to purchase a new car from the showroom. It was a reputed brand and the dealer was honest. In the normal course of events, if he would have gone straight to the showroom, he would have been given a decent vehicle and all would have ended well. But this industrialist decided to gild the lily. He made a phone call to the showroom impersonating a local minister and made a recommendation that so-and-so should be taken care of and the best of the vehicles should be delivered to him. The car was delivered. The industrialist was satisfied. A few days later, the dealer called the minister and assured him that he had taken good care of the industrialist and also offered to be of assistance in future if the minister needed him. The minister was first surprised because he had made no such call. And then he became really annoyed. He lodged a police complaint against the industrialist who had to spend a few days in prison before he got bail.

> *Many times we are too impatient to allow things to happen. We try to fast-forward things which boomerangs on us. You cannot pull out a tree each day and see how big its roots have grown.*

This was a classic case of gilding the lily. A lily in itself is pretty. There is absolutely no need of spraying gold paint on it. We find a lot of such situations in real life. The more we fuss about something, the more are the chances of things going wrong.

Religion and rituals

There is more of superstition than devotion in most religions. The rituals and dogmas in most cases have deviated the people practicing various religions from their very purpose. Religion and faith means a surrender in totality.

A true faith demands total devotion and absolute surrender which most often gets diluted in dogmas and rituals. This short story about Majnu illustrates this point.

Majnu is an immortal lover whose love for his Laila made him almost mad. In a demented state he was running around searching for his Laila. A few faithful and devout Muslims were facing towards the west and performing their Namaaz. It is said that one should not walk across a person doing his Namaaz. But Majnu was so dazed and demented in his thoughts about Laila that he walked across nevertheless.

Rituals are no substitute for true devotion and surrender to the will of God. God places more emphasis on righteous conduct than on rituals.

The moment he crossed the faithful doing Namaaz, one of the devout Muslims got really irritated. Leaving his prayers half way through, he ran after Majnu, pounced on him and started beating him. It took a few moments for Majnu to realise why he was being beaten. He then said, "Laila is after all a mortal. Yet so immersed was I in thoughts of her that I did not see you praying. However, it is strange that you, who should have been fully immersed in God, have so wavering a mind that your interest is not in your prayers but on seeing who walks across while you pray."

If you read through the whole of the Quran, you would not find even at one place the method of offering the Namaaz. The good lord has left it to us to decide on our own methods of prayers. But in the current times, for an ordinary Muslim, the rituals of Namaaz have superceded the teachings of the Quran.

Amongst Hindus I have seen a similar fervour while organising and performing various rituals and ceremonies. The ritual becomes so important that it takes away the purpose of God and religion. The ignorant priest chanting Sanskrit *mantras,* the meanings of which he has absolutely no idea about, cannot be a guide who could lead you to God.

In my opinion, religion is an absolutely private business between you and your God. Only God needs to know how much you love, rever or respect him. Making a dance and drama about religious rituals makes you neither more religious nor close to God.

Pearl 46: Appropriate technology — when in snow, use a ski

Mohammed Bin Tughlaq was an emperor with eccentric ideas but well known as a patron of arts and a benevolent person. Each day he would receive a lot of people who would offer him gifts and respects. Once he had a perfumer from Persia who brought him a very tiny bottle of essence. He had to just open the lid when the whole palace was filled with a delectable perfume. The king was not a great connoisseur of perfumes but rewarded the Persian nevertheless with a hundred gold coins.

Later that day, a poor cobbler sought audience with the emperor. This cobbler had spent his entire fortune on purchasing leather belonging to a rare Afghan goat. He had ascertained the queen's foot size and had spent a whole year making a special shoe for the queen. It was really well stitched and would be worn proudly by the loftiest of the queens.

> *Whatever technology, whatever means, whatever methods you adopt in any walk of life, they must be appropriate to you.*

The cobbler made his presentation which was accompanied by loud cheers and claps by the assembled audience. Tughlaq too was happy and made an announcement:

"These shoes are really good and worth at least fifty gold coins if not more. Here, take this bottle of perfume. This comes all the way from Persia and I have paid a hundred gold coins for it."

The cobbler was too stunned to reply and walked back clutching the small phial tightly in his fist. The cobbler lived in abject poverty and thus could not find any use for the perfume.

A few days later he had to make another shoe but realised that he did not have the few drops of oil that would be needed for the thread. He had no option but to soak the thread in the perfume given by the king!

It was indeed the world's most powerful perfume and the moment the shoes were ready, the perfume spread so wildly that the smell reached even the palace. Tughlaq took a whiff of the air and summoned the cobbler who told him how he had put the perfume to use.

"You stupid fool! You spent a perfume worth a hundred gold coins to soak your sewing thread?"

The cobbler replied with a bent head:

"My Lord! For a poor man like me, it is only worth the oil it contains!"

PEARL 47: Tenacity and determination are keys to success

King Janaka was well-known both for his benevolence and wisdom. Once, he had to appoint a commander for his army. Six contenders of equal skills, qualifications and experience presented a difficult choice indeed. The king thought for a moment and said: "He who brings me a sieve full of water from the river will lead my armed forces." Those were the times before plastic meshes. Sieves were woven of split bamboo. The river was at a considerable distance and it appeared to be an almost impossible task to bring a sieve full of water. But the king's command had been unambiguous and they set out. Each time they filled up the bamboo sieve, it would empty before it was taken out of water. The first candidate gave up after a dozen attempts. In an hour, four more soldiers had realised the futility for the exercise and abandoned

> *One who hangs on even by the skin of his teeth shall be victorious.*

all efforts. The sixth guy, however, continued undeterred and unperturbed. By mid-day he realised that he could walk about a dozen yards before the water drained off. He did not know the reason, but was pleased that he was having some progress. Gradually he realised that repeated soaking in the water had swollen the bamboo strips and the sieve holes had started shrinking. Finally, by sunset, he was in Janaka's palace with a sieve full of water. The king gave an explanation: "I want my commander to be a persistent and tenacious person."

It was tenacity that helped Lord Rama to spend fourteen years in the jungle. It was tenacity that helped Nelson Mandela to spend a greater part of his life in prison and yet survive.

PEARL 48: Survivors avoid 'a holier-than-thou' person like the plague

Two celibate priests had to cross a river. As they approached the riverbank, they saw a poor girl attempting to cross the river. However, she slipped and sprained her ankle. When they approached the river, the poor girl was seated on a boulder, massaging her ankle. The first priest who took his vows seriously, did not even cast a glance at the girl. He was afraid of breaking his vows by even looking at the girl. The second priest, however, saw the helpless look in her eyes and unhesitatingly picked her up and carried her across on his shoulder. He dropped her on the opposite bank and they started on their way. They would have walked for about an hour when the first priest addressed his colleague, "The way the girl clung to your back, don't you think you have committed a sin carrying her across?" The second priest answered, "I have dropped the burden at the opposite bank. It is you who is still carrying it in your heart!"

> *A survivor does not allow the self-proclaimed guardians of morality to decide for him as to what is good and what is bad. Avoid them like the plague.*

This parable shows that it is the immoral people who act as the staunchest defenders of morality. Morality is a code of conduct for ourselves. It is for you and your conscience to decide what is moral and what is immoral.

PEARL 49 — One who invites trouble deserves it

A drunk Irishman was tossed out of the pub by the bouncers. As he fell down on the street, his face fell into a pile of dog droppings and he became unconscious. He recovered consciousness after some time and stood up shakily. He sniffed the air with distaste because all that he could smell was a blob of dog turd stuck to his nose.

He staggered into the bar once again and took a deep breath. He wrinkled his nose in distaste once again and walked out. A ten-minute walk had brought him to the main road. He took a deep breath again and said, "What a day! The whole world smells of shit!"

With the blob of dog turd pasted on his nose, it was no wonder that he smelled shit everywhere.

> For a survivor, the best way is to avoid trouble, rather than invite it.

We, too, on many occasions walk around with a lump of dog turd pasted to our nose and then scream that the whole world smells of shit. Examples abound of the numerous instances where the fault is ours but we blame the whole world for it.

Young ladies wearing revealing and provocative clothes is one example. No roadside Romeo would pass comments about a sensibly and modestly dressed young lady. But the moment she starts wearing micro skirts and blouses, cat calls, whistles and gropes automatically follow. Feminists would shout that they have a right to wear what they want. Yes! You do! You have a right to wear clothes as revealing as you want. Just as you have a right to walk around with a blob of shit pasted on your nose. But then please don't blame the whole world that it stinks.

Help only the truly deserving

I have mentioned earlier about help. It is a tenet that distinguishes a sentient being from a lesser developed animal. To help others is actually our duty. But two things are important. The person being helped should both <u>Desire</u> and <u>Deserve</u> the help. This anecdote is from mythology.

> *Help only the truly deserving ones. This will ensure that optimal use is made of your help.*

Frogs can swim, but a scorpion cannot. Incessant rains had caused floods and a drowning scorpion begged a frog to take it across.

"But if I carry you on my back, you would bite me," said the frog. The scorpion promised not to bite and boarded the frog's back as it swam across. Half way across, it bent down its tail and stung the frog.

The poison spread and the dying frog asked just as he sank:

"Oh scorpion! Why have you bitten me? Now both of us will drown!"

The drowning scorpion said, "I just can't help it. It is my nature, and just as you cannot stop helping others, I cannot stop stinging others!"

This parable clearly proves that help should only be offered to someone who deserves it.

Pearl 51: The power of positive thinking

A leading shoe manufacturer in America decided to expand its operation to Hawaii. The population was five million and the market appeared tremendous. However, the first sales person who was sent in panicked. He flew back the next day, and with a long face conveyed his disappointment:

"The place is full of undeveloped savages who do not wear shoes. We have no hopes at all!" The management did not want to give up so soon and sent another man. This chap sent a cable the next day: "Five million customers ready and waiting. Please rush stocks immediately."

> There is a beautiful prayer: *"God, grant me the serenity to accept the things that I cannot change; the courage to change the things that I can; and the wisdom to know the difference."*

Where the first salesman saw despondency and gloom, the second chap saw opportunities. While walking in Trafalgar Square if a flying pigeon shits on him, a pessimist would crib and moan about his ruined suit. An optimist would look heavenwards and say happily, "Oh God, thanks for not giving wings to elephants!"

Half a glass of water can either be seen as a glass <u>half-full</u> or as a glass <u>half-empty</u>. It all depends on the outlook of the viewer. It is a fact that things remain as they are, whether you like them or not. A survivor would adapt, change and move ahead, while a loser would crib and moan.

You hold your destiny

Chanakya was the most perceptive genius this land has ever produced. He was the brain behind the great Mauryan Empire. Before him, India was nothing but a group of small republics which fell easily under the onslaught of Alexander. In fact, it was under Chanakya's intelligent leadership that India was united for the first time and became a country. In his young age when he went to the *gurukul* to study, a lot of importance was given to palmistry and other facial signs known as *saamudrik shastra*. Before he could get admission, he was asked to show his palm to the teacher. After a thorough examination, the *guru* told him that he was unsuitable for education because his palm lacked the line of education. A curious Chanakya asked the *guru* as to where on the palm would one usually find such a line. The *guru* pointed to an appropriate area on his palm. Pulling out a knife, the boy Chanakya scored a deep gash on his palm and said, "Now I have a line. Let us start!"

> *Destiny applies only to those who do their karma. You cannot lay down your arms in the battlefield and expect victory. You have a right to expect victory only if you get up and fight as best as you can.*

This is what Lord Shri Krishna has also propounded in the Bhagavad Geeta. It is your bounden duty to do your *karma*. Leave the results to God. You are not allowed to sit idle and do nothing, claiming that whatever is destined for you, will happen.

Destiny

Our destiny is in our hands and in no one else's. If we believe that we can do it, we will definitely succeed. It is the weak who get disheartened when they face tough odds.

An elderly couple had a sixteen-year old daughter who suffered from a rare disease called brittle bone disease because the bones break at the least provocation. The young lady was my patient. During her childhood she had sustained so many fractures that her limbs appeared tortuous and twisted like a snake. As she grew older, the breaks became less frequent but the stigma of malunion existed in the form of twisty limbs. She walked slowly, carefully and with a limp because even at this age she could break her bones with a fall.

Her aim was to study medicine. In medical college admissions there is a quota for disabled candidates. A candidate with a physical disability of more than forty percent qualified for a relaxed admission criteria. I knew of her fierce determination to get into medicine and when she came to get her medical entrance examination forms attested, told her that I could issue her a disability certificate that would give her an admission in the disabled quota. I still remember her answer.

> *Once survivors decide, success has no business of eluding them.*

"Doctor uncle! Just because I am not physically perfect does not mean that I would settle for being a less than perfect doctor. I want to compete on my merits and if I don't succeed this year, I will appear the next. And the next year after that. I want to be shown no favours in selection and no favours in my exams. I want to be an excellent doctor like you!"

A few years later she come to my clinic with a box full of sweets. She had passed her MBBS and was now a fully qualified doctor. She had even got a medal!

PEARL 54: The importance of your social obligations

A kingdom once suffered from some calamity. The priests advised that a pond be filled with milk for bathing the presiding deity of the city and propitiating it. Each house in the kingdom was ordered to pour a bowl full of milk into the pond. By the following morning, the pond would be full of milk adequate for the rituals. A stingy trader told his wife, "I have found a way out. We will wait till late night and then pour a bowl of water. One bowl of water in so much milk would go unnoticed." He did exactly that.

> *Being a survivor does not mean being selfish. We survive in a society and not on an isolated island. We do have a responsibility towards the society. All of us need to contribute our bit.*

The next morning when the king got to the pond, he was surprised to see it full of water. Everyone in the kingdom had thought of the same thing!

Some reader could argue—what would have happened if others had poured milk and the trader would not have been caught?

The answer is that even if the whole city had poured milk and you had got away with pouring a bowl of water, you would not have really got away from your inner conscience which knew the truth.

As responsible members of our society, unless each one of us is honest to ourselves, how can our society progress?

PEARL 55 — If you can't lick them, join them

A drill sergeant faced a batch of fresh recruits; he stared hard at them and shouted in a booming voice, "I am Sergeant Smith. I am six foot three and weigh a hundred and ten kilos. Is there anyone out there who thinks that he can whip me?" From the back, a hand rose. This belonged to a black gentleman who was six foot six and weighed a hundred and twenty-five kilos. The sergeant walked briskly to him and grabbed him by the elbow. Dragging him to the front of the group he barked again, "Men! This is my new assistant. Now is there anyone who thinks that he can whip us both?"

This is a classic example of a profound tip for the survivor—if you can't lick them, join them. A survivor knows when to sue for peace. A survivor knows when to fight and when to retreat in the presence of overwhelming odds.

> *Conserve your energies for things more useful than fighting a system which you cannot change anyway.*

On many occasions, it may be better to retreat than to confront. Rather than be a romantic fool and lose your life today, it may be better to retreat and live enough to fight another day. Survivors avoid unnecessary confrontation. I am not suggesting that you should not fight for your ideals or whatever you hold sacred. I am not asking you to become a conformist either. You have to have a personality of your own, views of your own. But you should have the discrimination to correctly assess where opposing something is worthwhile and where it is not.

PEARL 56: Don't miss the macro picture for the micro picture

Smith and Jones were neighbours. They brought a horse each and to make sure that there was no confusion about who owned which horse, they snipped off half a tail of Smith's horse. The kids, who lived in the neighbourhood were a mischievous lot and in the night, trimmed the tail of the other horse too. Jones then cut his horse's right ear, but the boys too did the same. Bit by bit the horses lost body parts. Eventually, the frustrated friends sat musing in the bar: "Things have gone on a bit too much. Now is the time to stop else we would seriously damage our horses. We want a proper solution." A smart man interjected, "Well, it's simple! Smith, you keep the brown horse while Jones will keep the black one!"

> Survivors always have their vision focussed on the macro picture. One gets into the micro picture only when it is warranted. And then there are people to go into the micro picture for you at a cost.

Sometimes we are so occupied by micro details that we miss the big picture. You appreciate a great work of art only from a certain distance and not by standing very close to it. A good doctor diagnoses a patient's problem correctly only when he looks at the totality of symptoms. Many specialists suffer from this drawback. They are prone to paying more attention to some small thing of their speciality and miss the more troublesome complaints.

57. Don't let stupid rules and regulations make you stupid

A man had throat infection. It was so bad that he could barely speak. He went to a very busy doctor's clinic. The head nurse asked him to strip, wear a paper gown and wait in the adjoining room. He protested that he was having only a sore throat but the nurse would hear nothing. As he sat on the bench shivering in a paper gown, he looked at a youth sitting beside him and whined, "I just have a sore throat and she asks me to strip and wear a paper gown!" The boy gave a sardonic smile and said, "At least you are sick. I am the delivery boy who had come to deliver the courier and she has made me strip too!"

> *Survivors avoid falling into the trap of red tape as far as possible. Red tape has no mind. If you have one, avoid it.*

To avoid the doctor from wasting his time as the patient undressed, the clinic had a system that the patient was all ready before he got to the doctor. Leave it to an efficient nurse to carry the rules far enough. Another similar story by an army cadets tells it all.

The National Defence Academy had a lovely flower garden and the recruits were roistered for watering duties. They would be posted in groups of six and would spend from 04.30 hours to 06.30 hours watering the garden. Once, it was raining torrentially and the six cadets on watering duty thanked their stars and went to bed. When the drill sergeant came for an inspection at 06.00 hours and found them asleep, he was so angry that he not only awarded them a penalty but also insisted that they do the watering wearing their raincoats and mackintosh rubber boots!

Like the efficient nurse, the efficient drill sergeant had carried the rules a little too far. Many times we carry on the rules so far that their original purpose is lost.

PEARL 58 — Look for the real McCoy; don't get fooled by red herrings

Drunken driving is the fourth commonest cause of death the world over and developed countries have very strict laws against this. The incidents of drunken driving escalate during festivals and special police teams are posted at strategic points to catch the unwary.

A pub closed a little after midnight and people started coming out. One customer stumbled out and lurched so badly that he almost fell down. Somehow he recovered and staggered towards his vehicle. The two plainclothes policemen standing behind a parked pick-up van gave a wide smile as they watched his antics. They were in no hurry because they could not catch him until he actually got into the car and drove away. He took two steps and again stumbled. He reached his car but could not find his keys.

> *Survivors learn to avoid getting fooled by red herrings.*

After some struggle, he located the keys but could not locate the keyhole. It took him ten minutes to open the car and get in. The hidden cops watched in glee as the other customers got into their respective cars and drove away. The man took his own sweet time to fumble and eventually locate the ignition key. He struggled to start the vehicle and put the reverse gear by accident. The vehicle rolled back a few feet before he realised his mistake and screeched ahead.

In the normal course, he would have been allowed to drive a little on the main road before the cops chased and caught him. But in this case, he was too dangerous to be allowed to wreak havoc on the innocent pedestrians and other motorists. The two cops pounced on him and stopped the car. To their surprise he looked sober when he got out of the vehicle. They administered him a breath test which turned out to be NEGATIVE! They took him to the police station for a blood test and waited for half an hour for the test results. The blood alcohol turned out to be nil! A distraught sergeant asked him, "Sir, who are you?" With a smile he replied, "Well, sergeant, I am a professional decoy." The other patrons of the pub had got together and hired a professional decoy who would keep the cops busy so that the drunken drivers amongst them could escape undetected.

Pearl 59 — Learn to read between the lines

These days we are assailed by business offers, each more lucrative than the other. It would appear that the manufacturers have become charity organisations. Buy one take two; buy this, get that too, and so on. Is that really true? There has to be a catch somewhere.

A standard business trick is to insert the real catch either in fine print or couch it in undecipherable legal language. They are also known as routine clauses. These routine clauses are hidden things printed in microscopic letters at the end of the contract and are practically invisible, unless you are so knowledgeable that you specifically ask about them, or look at the print using magnifying glasses.

> *Survivors learn to recognise hidden liabilities before they fall on them.*

I had once gone to a seaside resort which has a lovely backwater lagoon and where boating is a wonderful experience. The boats are tiny plastic affairs with foot pedals and two seats. While I was paddling quietly, my boat shook as a speedboat whizzed by churning a huge wake. I looked up and saw a real beauty, a sleek fibreglass boat with a tilted windscreen and a 300 hp outboard motor. I was mesmerised by the boat and I too wanted to zip in one, like James Bond.

The thought of possessing a speed boat become an obsession with me. I found out the man and he turned out to be an NRI who was going back and was planning to sell the boat. In spite of vehement protests from my wife, I bought it for Rs. 5 lakh.

The fine print became clear only later. I could not park the boat at the jetty because it was a government jetty. If I had to take a permit, it would take six months and a heavy bribe! Meanwhile,

I had to thus park it in the berthing dock of a private club, the membership of which put me down by another couple of lakhs. Only after I started using it that I realised that it consumed sixty litres of petrol an hour, hardly an affordable expenditure. When the engine developed trouble after some time, it was found that the replacement could be had only from Singapore. At the end of six months I was so fed up that I had to sell it and that too at less than half the cost.

PEARL 60
Impulsiveness kills

This one is from the Jataka tales and has been repeated so often that anyone with our social background would have heard it. But it carries such an important message that it bears repeating once again!

As his parents had died when he was young, he had been brought up by his elder brother. Later when the elder brother married, it was the brother and sister-in-law who acted as his father and mother. The three of them lived happily and people used to comment upon the love and affection in the family. "It is almost like Rama, Sita and Lakshmana," the neighbours would comment.

> *The rule of thumb for the survivor is to react slowly but act fast.*

The younger returned home early one day with severe discomfort in his eye. A speck of dust or hair had gone into the eye and was irritating him. The elder brother had not yet come back and the younger fellow approached his sister-in-law for help. The lady tried wiping it and blowing on it but it did not work. Finally the lady sat down on the floor and the younger brother lay down with his head in her lap. She bent down to blow properly so that the particle would be blown away. It was at this time that the elder brother entered the house.

The spectacle he saw shocked him. He saw his brother lying on his wife's lap with her head bent forward, the two faces close to each other almost as if in a kiss! He lost his temper and pulled out the sword hanging from the wall. In a single swift stroke, he decapitated his wife and plunged the sword into his brother's heart. That was indeed the punishment for adultery in those times. The wife died instantly but the younger brother took some time to die. He cleared the misunderstanding just before he died. His sister-in-law was like a mother to him who was pulling out a fleck of dust.

Intelligence quotient

IQ or intelligence quotient is a highly misused concept. The concept of IQ was developed for kids or somewhat retarded people. People indiscriminately apply it in all walks of life. IQ is not synonymous with achievement in life. Human society as it is today, owes most of its development to some great inventions and discoveries like electricity, electronics and so on. They were made by people who, in their childhood, were not very high IQ children. On the other hand, they were hard-working dedicated people. Creativity is the result of both intelligence and diligence. Real achievers use a judicious mix of both. If something can be done by intelligence alone, they do it. If it cannot be done by intelligence, they use diligence or sheer hard labour to do it.

> *Survivors take what comes to them naturally and make the most of it; what they don't get naturally, they make up by dint of sheer hard work.*

Mozart was a genius. In his very short life, he composed nearly a 100 symphonies. He depended only on talent or intelligence. Beethoven, on the other hand, was not blessed with such natural talent and took nearly 10 years to compose one symphony. It was sheer hard work. But his creations are no less great. Not all high IQ people are a social or economic success. Bill Gates was no genius as a student. Many of the great industrialists like Dhirubhai Ambani did not have degrees from Harvard and had started as small traders only.

The point common to all achievers is that they were dedicated to their work.

PEARL 62 — Think before you pay in advance

A tourist in Madrid went to a local restaurant. Being a snob, he wanted to try the costliest dish, but the manager apologetically explained that he could not have the dish on that day because it was sold out.

"So make some more! I will wait as long as it takes!"

"But that is not possible, Sir! The special dish is fried bull testicles in a special Italian sauce. Only one bull dies a day. Today's dish is already booked for and paid in advance!"

> *Survivors avoid paying in advance.*

The snobbish tourist pulled out his wallet and paid for the next five days in advance. The next day he was served the dish. It tasted good. On the fourth day he was in for a surprise. That day, the testicles were small, shrivelled and tasted awful. While he was trying to chew it, he called the restaurant owner and complained. The manager explained, "It is not always that the bull loses, some times it wins too, Senor!"

Most of us have faced such situations in life when we have to compromise under certain circumstances and feel cheated.

63 In the poker of life don't play blind

Don't make a promise which you cannot keep. And don't make a promise in the hope that the condition which you place for the promise is impossibly difficult. Sometimes impossible becomes possible. Hindi films are fond of a theme where a poor boy falls in love with a rich girl and the girl's father imposes a condition that unless the boy earned so much in so much time, he can't even see the girl. The boy, of course, does it by hook or by crook.

Rare though such instances may be, they do happen in real life. The son of Hiram Maxim, the inventor of the machine gun, recalls that once as a child, he had gone to a huge store and the shopkeeper had jokingly told him that if he could bring a dollar with heads on both sides, he could have anything from the store for free. Maxim took two dollars, filed away half the thickness from both of them and then joined them. The store owner had to eat humble pie before the ingenuity of this great inventor.

> *Survivors are not found on the wrong end of such promises. Before making an unsafe bet, make sure that you can fulfil it if you lost!*

Pearl 64: Accept your limitations and be happy with them

A young mother got into a London bus carrying her tiny wrapped-up baby. Small babies either look really cute or obnoxiously hideous. But this one was a little worse than that. So much so that when the conductor came to her for tickets, he looked at the child and said:

> Be happy with what is given to you and tell those people who laugh at you that Napoleon was a short man and Cleopatra was a plain-looking woman.

"Madam! This is carrying it too far. I have seen all sorts of babies in this bus. However, I have seen none so ugly as this!"

The young mother was livid with rage. She was in tears, found a bench on the foot path and sat down with the baby, and as she continued to weep, an elderly gentlemen walked by. He saw the damsel in distress and nodded sagely. Walking to a pub across the street, he got a glass of brandy. He addressed the girl:

"Now, now, don't cry. Whatever it is, this brandy will settle it. And I have even got some peanuts for the monkey!"

Let us face the facts. There are certain things that we have to accept. If you have stopped growing at five and a half feet, no amount of Complan or hanging by the parallel bars would make you taller. The elevator shoes might help you, but barefooted you are back to truth!

Our problem starts when we cannot accept our limitations. Now there are two types of handicap—one that you can overcome, and the other you cannot. If you don't know a language or the use of computers, you can overcome the handicap by learning it. But if you have a dark complexion, even tons of Fair and Lovely would not work. Had it been working, there would have been no dark-complexioned girl in India by now.

65 Bad luck is bad luck, accept it

Joseph fell down from a ladder and broke his thigh. Encased in a huge plaster he had to spend the next twelve weeks in bed. With nothing to do, boredom was killing him. A week later he saw an ant. He got an idea and caught the ant. He kept it in a match box and made it his pet. He fed it sugar cubes and decided to teach it tricks. It was a slow and painful work but Joseph had all the time in the world.

He made matchstick barriers which he taught the ant to jump across. He built small puddles with saucers of water and the ant demonstrated breast stroke and underwater swims.

> *Take it easy. As the saying goes: Dil par mat le, yaar!*

As a climax he would build a fire wall with broken matchsticks which the ant would glide through majestically. Twelve weeks later the plaster come off and Joseph was anxious to find an audience who would appreciate his circus ant. Carrying the insect in his pocket, he went to a bar in which cousin Tony was the barman. Joseph ordered for a beer and as Tony came back with the glass, he opened his matchbox and let out the ant.

"Hey Tony! See the ant here?"

"Oops, Sorry Joseph."

The palm came down smack, splattered the ant and tossed it away.

"Now Joseph! Tell me how you spent the last three months?"

It happens to all of us some time or the other. We sweat our blood to plan and prepare something but at the last moment things go wrong denying us our rightful credit. The unexpected anticlimax leaves us too stunned to react.

Upgrades and upgradation

In a remote part of Africa where civilisation was yet to reach, a cannibal and his young son went out to get some food. They left the deep woods and came to a village. With spears in hand, they waited behind the bushes for a victim. After a short while a shrivelled old lady walked by. The son tapped his dad's shoulders and whispered, "Dad! Shall I spear her?" The man shook his head from one side to another. "No, son! Her meat is too skimpy and would be really tough to eat. The bones would be hollow with no marrow. Let us wait a while till something tastier comes along."

> *Survivors avoid such unnecessary expenditures.*

An hour later an obese lady walked by. She was really plump and roly-poly. The son tapped his father's shoulder but the cannibal refused as he whispered back, "No son! Too much of fat. This cholesterol thing is really bad for our heart. Would actually clog our arteries if we eat a tub of lard like this!"

They waited for another hour and then she came. An American tourist. A blonde with a smashing figure and a video camera around her neck. The shapely legs that showed out of the skirt left no doubt that she was all toned muscle without an ounce of fat. The son realised that this was one about whom his father would have no objection. "Dad! She is perfect. Come let's spear her!"

The cannibal shook his head again and said, "No son! I have a better idea. Let us take her home and cook your mother instead."

In layman's terms, this would be what we call upgradation. A Pentium IV to a Pentium V, Windows 98 to a Windows 2001, a pager to a cellular phone! This year's model with last year's car. With a quest for the fastest, best and latest, sometimes we forget the value of old things that really work. Henry Ford had once said "Why fix a machine if it has not gone wrong?"

Lakshmana Rekha

Ramayana is an immortal epic originally rendered by Valmiki and then retold in all local languages by various poets. An important episode in this classic is about Sita's abduction and the Lakshmana Rekha. The story goes like this:

Rama, his wife Seeta and brother Lakshmana were forced to spend fourteen years in the forests. Seeta was a pretty lady and Ravana, the king of neighbouring Sri Lanka wanted to kidnap her. He sent his *rakshasa* Mareecha disguised as a golden deer to tempt Seeta. Seeta, fascinated by it, begged of Rama to get her the deer which she desired to have as a pet. Rama was worried to leave his wife alone and thus instructed Lakshmana to stay back and look after his sister-in-law.

> *A survivor knows that the Lakshmana Rekha in the form of social or moral restrictions is not to restrict your freedom of action but to keep troubles at bay—cross the Lakshman Rekha and you will be doing it at your own risk.*

Mareecha led Rama on a chase and having drawn him far away screamed out in a loud voice, which sounded like Rama's scream of anguish. Seeta, who heard the sound, was justifiably anxious and implored Lakshmana to go in search of Rama. The younger brother was a little reluctant because he had been instructed by Rama to stay behind and stand guard. But Seeta insisted that Lakshmana should rush immediately to offer assistance.

Lakshmana left but not before drawing a line outside the door, a few feet away. Pointing to the line, he told Seeta that he had chanted special prayers so that no outsider would be able to cross the line and reach her. This Lakshman Rekha would offer her protection. He forbade Seeta from crossing the line and then went in search of Rama.

Ravana, who was waiting for some such opportunity, came in the guise of a Brahmin. Seeta handed him alms across the line, but the moment her hand crossed the safe barrier, he held it and pulled her across. Once Seeta was on the other side of the line, nothing could be done to protect her from being kidnapped. This one act of inadvertently crossing the Lakshmana Rekha produced great anguish for everyone and resulted in a major war.

PEARL 68

Selective delusions

The lion approached a jackal and roared, "Who is the king of the jungle?" "You, Master!" came a meek reply. He walked ahead haughtily and asked the deer and the hyena, and the boar and the monkey. They all gave the same answer. A little ahead, he saw the elephant standing under a tree.

"Who is the king of the jungle?"

The elephant gave one disdainful look and gave but a big kick. The lion was flung many feet in the air and fell down with a thump.

Survivors don't have any delusions about themselves or any other thing.

Dusting himself, the lion said, "Just because you don't know the answer, you mustn't go around kicking people!"

Similar in message is a man making a statement:

"I am not afraid of my wife. I don't have to ask her before I do anything. For example, I have even taken her permission to make the above statement!"

People are selectively delusional about certain things and would never change their opinion even if the evidence is to the contrary. Examples of the selective delusions that delude most of us are:

1. Husband is the master of the house.
2. My children listen to me and I get them only things that I want.
3. Our vote is a powerful weapon.
4. Politicians are honest.
5. The police is there to protect the poor and innocent against the rich and powerful.

6. Judges are not corrupt.
7. Our country is developing.
8. Big dams are good for a nation.
9. A high stock market index is a sign of healthy economy.
10. Your subordinate really respects you.

In many cases it is like a husband who doesn't need his wife's permission or the lion that knows well that he is the king of the jungle.

Prepare for the indirect consequences too

This one is from Texas. A newly married farmer drove his bride dressed in bridal whites in a lovely horse carriage drawn by a magnificent white horse. As the carriage got out of the church, the horse trotted towards a small ditch and the vehicle lurched dangerously. "First warning!" said the groom softly as he cracked the whip. A little later came another hole and the carriage bumped once again. "Second warning," he said as he cracked the whip. Unfortunately, the carriage ran over a third hole too. The farmer got down and shot his horse. Blowing at the barrel of his gun he said softly, "I don't give third warnings!"

> *The shooting of the horse produced an entirely different consequence. Similarly, many consequences are indirect. Survivors prepare for them.*

The wife jumped down and looked at the magnificent animal lying dead. She shouted in anger, "How could you have done this? To shoot such an expensive horse! And now we will have to walk all the way." The farmer looked hard at his wife and softly said, "First warning."

They remained happily married for the next forty years, without a quarrel.

PEARL 70: Money is important, but not all that important

A young and successful lawyer in the US parked his car and got out. It was a brand new Porsche and looked great. He had just opened the door when a pick-up van sped by crashing into the door and wrenching if off its hinge. The lawyer was terribly upset to see such a horrible mutilation to his car. He got out and stood, looking sadly at his car. His pastor friend who was driving by got down. The young lawyer wailed, "That bastard! Never even stopped. See how he has wrenched my door so horribly!"

The pastor looked at the fallen door and then looked at a wrenched off arm lying beside it, all bloody. The priest got a shock and admonished the lawyer. "You are so much of a materialist! You have not even noticed that your arm has been wrenched off. All you are bothered about is your car and door!" The lawyer looked at his bloodied stump and let out another loud moan: "Oh, no! My brand new Rado watch!"

> Money is important, no doubt, but it is not everything.

In the materialistic society we live in, we are so enamoured by wealth and creature comforts that we reach a mistaken conclusion that money is almost everything. As Kalidas has said: "Money can buy you silk cushions and soft beds but money can't buy you sleep. Money can buy you the best food but money can't buy you hunger. Money could buy a hundred things to make you happy but money cannot buy you happiness." It is so very true even now.

71 Confidence is good, over-confidence is bad

A smart and aggressive salesman drove his van to a place in Bihar. He landed in front of a house, and carrying the vacuum cleaner, he knocked on the door. An old lady opened the door. He gave her a smile and started, "I am here to demonstrate my vacuum cleaner!" "But!!....."

"No buts! No ifs! This is the best vacuum cleaner in India."

"I agree with you but ..."

"No buts and ifs! You see this plastic bucket in my hand? It is full of cow dung and street dirt!"

> *Over-confidence is bad; survivors know it.*

"B...but..."

"No buts...! I am now going to sprinkle this all over your carpet and stamp over it like this!"

"B...but!"

"I know! You are angry at the carpet getting soiled! But don't you worry! My vacuum cleaner will suck it all out and make your carpet brand new!"

"But..."

"No buts! No ifs! If my machine doesn't clean every bit of dust, then I would lick it clean with my tongue!"

"But..."

"Instead of wasting time interrupting me, it would be better if you show me the plug point where I can insert this plug."

"But that is what I am trying to tell you. We don't have electricity supply!"

PEARL 72

The value of experience

This one is from the English countryside. Two bulls stood on the hilltop gazing at the vast meadow. They spotted a shepherd herding a hundred cows that were let loose for grazing. "Let us rush down and mate with a few of them!" snorted the younger bull. The older bull gave a languid look to the horizon and said softly, "No hurry, chum. Let us walk down and mate with *all* of them!"

> *Everyone likes to give advice and you can get the best advice for free.*

That is the difference between impetuous youth and the wisdom of experience. We waste all our energy in rushing ahead so that by the time we reach the end of the road, we are too tired to do what we set out to do in the first place.

Enthusiasm and talent by themselves are useless unless they are properly channellised by knowledge and wisdom, which most often comes with experience.

Until we have a sufficiently large pool of experiences of our own, it is advisable to take advice from people more experienced than us. You need not follow an advice blindly, but it sure works as a pointer or test bed.

Ingenuity

A newspaper's classified advertisement section carried a small advertisement:

"Unique mosquito killing machine. 100% effective, kills each and every mosquito. No replacements, no coils to burn, no creams to apply, no electricity expenses. No mats, no nets. Guaranteed to kill mosquitoes. Send a money order of Rs.100/- to the following address."

And once you sent the money, you would get a parcel. This would contain two flat stone tablets and a short instruction sheet.

Objectionable though these ads may be, the fact remains that they are highly ingenious and have indeed helped in boosting sales.

Place mosquito on one stone and hit with the other stone for a guaranteed kill. It is recommended that the stones be washed with warm water once a week.

One must admire the ingenuity of the advertiser whose product performed exactly as advertised. He had not made a single false claim while selling his two stones worth five rupees. We face this situation frequently in our day-to-day existence.

A shampoo advertises that it makes the hair ten times stronger. Another promises a 75% reduction in hair fall. A balding man could continue using the shampoo and never go bald. The toothpaste that kills 200% more germs. They do not tell you 200% more germs than what? And this ingenuity is manifest not only in describing a product but its uses as well.

Fishing lines work as excellent surgical sutures. Coca Cola is an excellent toilet cleaner. (No, Pepsi has not given me a commission, nor have they promised to buy a million copies to make this book a bestseller. It is just that Coke cleans a toilet better than Pepsi). A crushed cigarette rubbed on your wind shield acts as the best glass wipe.

74. Become what you think you are

A farmer's young boy found an eagle egg in its nest and brought it home. It was kept under a hen to allow it to hatch. The eaglet hatched along with the chicks and adapted all the habits of the chicks.

In another instance, a pregnant mongrel died in the forests delivering six pups. Five of the pups died of starvation but the sixth was a survivor. Despite its small size, it fiercely surged ahead into the dense forests in search of something to eat. In the clearing it saw a lioness lying languidly, three hungry lion cubs suckling its teats. The little doggie was very hungry, rushed ahead and put its mouth to a teat. The lazy sleepy lioness did not realise it at that time. Later, when she saw the tiny scrawny mongrel, she felt a surge of maternal pity and allowed it to continue to drink its milk. The pup thus grew in the jungle with the lion cubs, imitating them in all aspects. After some time, though the dog stopped growing in size, it continued to grow in courage as it played and grew up with the cubs who had now approached adulthood. One day, a team of wildlife photographers took position to shoot a video of the lions attacking a deer. In a dramatic documentary they captured the wild dog charge at the deer, jump on its back and dig its teeth into it's neck. The wildlife photographers never knew that though they considered it a dog, as far as the dog was concerned, it thought of itself to be a lion.

> *In real life too, we are only what we think we are!*

PEARL 75 — Even copying demands brains

A carpenter's son was insistent that his father carved some toys for him. When the wood was procured, the son wanted a 'wok' to be made (A wok is like a deep frying pan used by Chinese cuisine chefs as a utensil for deep frying and boiling). The father painstakingly carved a wooden wok which looked as good as the original. The son was happy and took it to the kitchen where he hung it with other utensils.

While the other utensils were used daily and would get sooty, grimy and dirty, the wooden wok remained unused and thus new. It would always boast about its cleanliness and newness. The other utensils too were in the wooden wok's awe because they realised that this was one utensil that was never used. Once, the little son was curious and decided to try heating some oil in the wooden wok. The oil soaked wood was such a highly combustible combination that the whole thing caught fire and burnt to cinders.

> *A survivor knows whom to copy, what to copy, whom not to copy and what not to copy.*

This ancient Chinese parable tells us a message similar to what we have heard in the Jataka tales about a jackal in a lion's skin. By enveloping himself in a lion skin, a jackal does not become a lion, just as being carved in the shape of a utensil doesn't make wood a sturdy wok.

Impossible to please

This one is for the ladies. A store that sells new husbands has just opened in New York City, where a woman may go to choose a husband. Among the instructions at the entrance is a description of how the store operates. There are six floors and the attributes of the men increase as the shopper ascends the flights. There is, however, a catch: you may choose any man from a particular floor, or you may choose to go up a floor, but you cannot go back down except to exit the building!

A woman goes to the Husband Store to find a husband. On the first floor the sign on the door reads—Floor 1: These men have jobs. The second floor sign reads—Floor 2: These men have jobs and love kids. The third floor sign reads— Floor 3: These men have jobs, love kids, and are extremely good-looking.

> *I want the ladies to change themselves in such a manner that they are saved from such allegations.*

"Wow," she thinks, but feels compelled to keep going.

She goes to the fourth floor and the sign reads—Floor 4: These men have jobs, love kids, are drop-dead good-looking and help with the housework.

"Oh, mercy me!" she exclaims, "I can hardly stand it!" Still, she goes to the fifth floor and the sign reads—Floor 5: These men have jobs, love kids, are drop-dead gorgeous, help with the housework, and have a strong romantic streak. She is so tempted to stay, but she goes to the sixth floor and the sign reads—Floor 6: You are visitor number 31,456,012 to this floor. There are no men on this floor. This floor exists solely as proof that women are impossible to please.

Work is worship

This one is from Veda Vyasa's narration in the Mahabharata.

Kaushika was a devout Brahmin youth who set out in a spiritual quest leaving his elderly parents at home. He learnt the four *Vedas* and all the *Puranas*. He devoted his time in prayers and austerities. Once he was sitting under a tree meditating when a crane sitting on that tree defiled him by its droppings. Kaushika looked at the bird angrily and in an instant, the crane fell down dead! The power of his own penance made him somewhat arrogant.

A little later he went to a Brahmin's house to beg for alms. The lady of the house was occupied in domestic chores and respectfully asked him to wait for a little while till she finished her work. Just then the husband returned home tired and hungry, and the housewife had to attend to his needs which took some time.

> *Lord Shri Krishna says:*
> *One can achieve as much perfection by the worship of God as he can by diligent performance of his own duties.*

Kaushika was made to wait for a long time. This angered him and he stared at her with blazing eyes as she came later with his food. With an innocent smile the lady admonished him:

"I am no crane to burn by your wrath. Looking after my husband is my first duty and it is this that has delayed me."

The sage was surprised how this woman could know what had transpired in the jungle. Suitably chastised he apologised to her and asked her as to how she knew. She asked him to go to Mithila and meet a person named Dharma Vyadha who would teach him things that he ought to know. Kaushika left for Mithila in search of Dharma Vyadha. He expected him to be living in a hermitage under peaceful surroundings.

However when he asked for directions, he was pointed to a butcher's shop and was shocked to see that the butcher behind the counter was none else but Dharma Vyadha. He stood there with revulsion when the butcher spotted him and said:

"Has that good Brahmin lady sent you? I will be happy to teach you what you have come to learn."

This surprised Kaushika again and he nodded his head silently. The butcher put away his tools of trade, washed himself and took the sage to his house. He made the sage wait while he tended the needs of his elderly parents. By the time he came out, Kaushika's education was complete! Even before the butcher could open his mouth Kaushika said, "Oh Dharma Vyadha! I now understand. There is no devotion like duty. And no worship like work. He who is a *Karma Yogi* and does his duty is practicing the best religion. What use is my chanting the *Vedas* in the jungle when my old parents are being neglected? I have understood you and today I leave to go back to my parents. My deity and devotion, work and worship is to look after them in their old age!"

There is always a third option

Two surgeons were taking a morning stroll and saw a man limping in a characteristic manner. The first surgeon said:

"I bet that it is a Coxa Vara. His damaged hip is making him limp in such a characteristic manner!" The second surgeon disagreed. He said: "No! You are wrong. He has Genu Valgus. The problem is in his knee and that is what makes him limp like this!" They decided to walk to him and ask him. The man replied, "It is neither my hip nor my knee. It is my torn slipper. I am walking this way so that it does not fall off!"

As I said earlier, education is to open up your mind, not to close it. A survivor keeps his eyes and ears open and his mind willing to admit even unconventional things when they are reasonable or compelling.

> *A survivor always looks for the third option. He is not mentally straitjacketed or bound by what he has been taught.*

The parable clearly illustrates the third option! A survivor always looks for the third option. When faced with two equally difficult choices, a little thought would easily provide a third very different but highly acceptable option!

The marketing team of Ciba Geigy found this out to their great advantage. Tooth-paste is a product with a high profit margin and a phenomenal consumption worldwide. Even a 1% increase in the market share would mean a difference of millions of dollars.

Ciba's brand was Binaca which faced tough competition from Colgate and Pepsodent. Each brand had its own loyalty and it was turning out to be practically impossible to snatch even a half percent sale from the competitors. Gimmicks like improved flavour, free gifts and increasing the quantity of paste per tube were tried but the loyalty was fierce and market share constant. The Ciba marketing team came out with a simple but indigenous third approach–to increase the diameter of the nozzle by twenty percent. The logic was simple. Each squeeze would eject 20% more tooth-paste. The trick worked and the sales improved by 6%. Though the customer base remained the same, the per customer usage had jumped producing a dramatic sales increase. Soon the other companies too did the same and now if you look at tooth-pastes, you would find that irrespective of the tube size, the nozzle size is the same. Extra large.

A study by Indian Dental Association showed that the present paste tubes ensured that we squeezed out two to three times the tooth-paste required for a proper brushing. And this revolutionary technique resulting in a dramatic sales increase came about by thinking about the third option!

It always pays to look around. A third option may suggest itself to you. It may turn out that it was neither a damaged hip nor a knee. It was a broken slipper!

Pearl 79: Get quickly to the crux of the matter

"Son, get up! It is already 7.30 a.m. Time to get ready for school!"

"Aw, Dad! I am sick and tired of it. Can I take an off at least for one day?"

"No, son! You have a new excuse each day. What is it today?"

"Well, Dad! I am sick and tired of school. I hate the punks there. And how long have I to continue to go to school?"

"Well, son, three answers. You have a duty to perform. Secondly, because you are the Principal. Thirdly, because you are forty-five years old, I think that you have to continue going for many more years to come!"

> *You don't have to be rude but don't waste time in unnecessary social pleasantries with strangers. Get to the point quickly.*

Time is precious. Many people fail to achieve simply because they waste a great deal of time. Survivors don't waste time. If someone comes to you with an appointment, the purpose of their visit is already known, so get to the point straightaway. But if it is a visitor without an appointment, don't waste time talking about the weather till you reach the crux of the matter.

PEARL 80: Use consultants, but don't let them take you for a ride

The fox invited the stork home for dinner. The milk was served in two shallow plates. While the stork stood by helplessly, the fox licked his plate clean. He then said, "Oh stork! I think you are not hungry. Let us not waste the milk. I will drink it." So saying, he slurped the second plate too. The stork stood by helplessly.

The stork felt insulted and decided to take revenge. It went to a consultant who charged an appropriate fee and gave the idea. When the fox was invited for dinner, the milk would be served in long-necked pitchers. The stork's long beak would go in but the fox would stand by helplessly. The happy crane extended an invitation.

> *Consultants have their own jargon which may sound awesome and impressive to the uninitiated. Make it a point to make the consultant repeat everything in simple language. You are paying him to help you, not to get confused by his jargon. You want practical solutions from him, not an academic discourse—you don't have to submit a thesis.*

The fox suspected some foul play and consulted the same consultant, who collected a fee and gave him an idea. With a bag dangling on his shoulder, the fox went to the stork's house the next day. The stork welcomed him with a smile and brought two long-necked pitchers full of milk. The stork hastily put its beak in and started drinking the milk. It had expected the fox to stand by helplessly but was surprised to see that the fox had opened its bag which was full of marbles.

One by one the marbles were dropped in while the level of milk rose up. Finally it brimmed to the top and the fox started slurping it with glee!

Consultants do a simple thing. They take your money and give you advice. Note that they don't sell you their loyalty. Tomorrow they would offer the very same advice to your competitor also for an appropriate fee! Remember, once you allow a consultant into your organisation, you make him privy to all your secrets, professional ethics may be damned. What can you do if he tells your secrets to your competitors? I would advise you to use consultants for only one reason. Ask them if they have taken up an assignment on behalf of your competitor. If yes, then pay the consultant not to learn how to improve your efficiency, but to learn your competitors' secrets!

Club membership

Membership to clubs is an activity which is associated with a lot of snob value. The place is exclusive, you get to sign your bills and most importantly the bills are really affordable. Compared to a five star hotel, the bills in a club would be about a quarter. But if you are not a regular club patron, it is not a good economic deal at all. The interest costs on your initial joining fee and non refundable deposit would offset the bill difference.

> *There is no need to apply all sorts of 'source' to get the membership of an elite club—better go to a five-star hotel.*

Once the financial situation is equalled, there is not much of a difference between a five star hotel and your own club except for snob value. We all encounter a situation in life where we have to entertain folks for lunch or dinner. I have developed my own technique of converting any five star hotel into your own personal club. I have used this technique on numerous occasions with excellent results.

Here is what I do. One day prior to the engagement, I visit the hotel. I meet the *maitre d'* and explain that I am expecting some special friends and expected excellent service. I not only reserve the table but choose the arrangement as well. I then ask them to swipe my credit card and I sign the charge slip. Five star hotels won't cheat you and you can leave a blank signed slip without fear.

I then give a handsome advance tip and also instruct them to add ten percent tip to the final bill. I check on the menu and locate the favourites. I have a rough rehearsal with the *maitre d'* before I leave. The next day when I take my guests, the hotel becomes my special club.

The *maitre d'* recognises me and welcomes me personally. The waiter who would be serving on my table seems to know me personally. The service is excellent. The food is superb. There are no unexpected surprises. And the best part is that I am not presented a bill. They will mail it to me with a copy of my filled in charge slip for my records. Even in a club, you have to sign a charge slip. If this doesn't impress your guests, tell me what will?

And the good thing about this scheme is that it would work in any town or city, not necessarily your hometown. Imagine doing this to your friend, or associate in his town! Won't he be zapped?

PEARL 82: One should take calculated risks, but not needless ones

A white man had gone to Africa as a tourist. He saw a lovely lake between two villages. The water was tempting. He took off his clothes and took a clean dive. Effortlessly, he swam across to the opposite side where he was greeted by a group of villagers who gazed at him in open-mouthed amazement. The moment he climbed up on the opposite bank, the locals started clapping vigorously and chanted, "White man's powerful magic!" "White man's mighty magic!"

The tourist was flattered but hastened to correct them. "It is no magic. It is called butterfly stroke. It is not difficult at all. I can even teach you how to swim butterfly strokes!"

> *A survivor takes only calculated risks and never needless ones. A survivor is a responsible person—he is not a kid who eats a bunch of green chillies to impress the girl next door.*

The chief said in a respectful voice, "Oh Sir! Butterfly stroke, breast stroke, free stroke, we know it all. But it needs a white man's magic to plunge into a pond with a hundred crocodiles and escape without a scratch."

The white man spent the whole day searching a way to go round the lake to fetch his clothes!

PEARL 83 — Look for the right man for the job

A gunner in the Second World War got a couple of medals for bravery. But he was getting deaf due to the explosions and noises. He decided to take up a law degree so that he would get a desk job away from the noise of the guns and artillery. He passed the written examination but failed in the physicals. His distance vision was not good enough to allow him admission into law college!

> Never ignore someone's natural aptitude.

And to imagine that he had got all his medals by shooting at distant targets! He was denied admission on the grounds that it is possible that he may not recognise the judge's face from the podium.

In real life too, situations make persons competent in a particular job though they have never been originally trained to do it. This is a true story about a Senior Neurosurgeon Late. Prof. Narendran. He installed a C.T. Scanner in his hospital and a technician was employed at a high salary. Appu was the Professor's chauffer and was always in the C.T. room when he was not driving the car.

One day the C.T. technician was unexpectedly absent and Appu offered to take the scan. The Professor decided to give him a chance and the scan came out better than what the technician had been dooing. It was all a matter of tilting the gantry which Appu, as a car mechanic, could visualise in three dimensions. And so, like the gunner, Appu too became an indispensable C.T. technician with no qualifications.

Certain people suddenly find a vocation that suits them. This may be at variance with their academics or what they were trained for. But once they find their niche, it is best that they stick to it!

PEARL 84
When the jab slips, land a hook

A couple of college kids were in a cinema hall. A few seats ahead of them sat a bald man whose polished skull was temptingly beckoning the students. John was the naughtiest of the lot and bet a ten-pound wager that he would tap the head. He walked to the bald man, gave a resounding slap and said, "Oh Archibald Lewinthoff! How have you been?" The bald man looked back and growled that he was not Archibald Lewinthoff. John got back to his seat and collected his ten pounds. His friends told him that if he could do it again, he would be paid fifty pounds. John walked back again and gave another resounding slap. In a loud voice, he said, "Archibald Lewinthoff. You can't fool me by lying that it is not you! I know that it is you!" The bald man gave a grunt and walked away. As John got back to collect his fifty pounds, they could see the bald man walk away to the opposite corner of the cinema hall and take a seat far away from them. "I bet you a hundred pounds that you cannot tap him again!" said his friend. Nodding his head, John walked down the aisle. Slowly he crept behind the bald man. He gave a resounding slap and shouted, "Oh Archibald Lewinthoff! You are here! I have mistakenly slapped another bald man twice. Poor fellow!"

> *What it would mean is that though it would appear as if the last drop from the lime has been squeezed, a slight shift in the technique can get a little more.*

In this funny story, there is an important management principle called "Appropriate Variance". All you need is a variation in the technique to achieve the little extra. We Indians know how to tilt the empty LPG cylinder to get gas for at least ten more minutes.

Tough times don't last, tough guys do

This is an incident by James Stillwell.

The captain of the plane was in a hurry to fly out of an airbase in Thule, Greenland. But everything was working against him. The truck to pump sewage from the plane was late, and then the airman pumping out the sewage was taking his own time. The irritated captain shouted:

"Hurry up airman else ………."

The man looked up and said:

"I have no stripes on my arm, it is forty degrees below zero, I am stationed in Thule, my truck is causing mechanical problems, and I am pumping sewage out of aeroplanes. Just how do you plan on punishing me?"

> *It doesn't matter how low you are feeling it is not going to be there for the rest of your life. Just refuse to give up.*

Most of us feel like this at some stage or the other in our lives. When things are low and it would appear that they could not get any lower they take yet another turn for the worse.

If you are ever feeling low having failed in your projects, have a look at the career graph of Abraham Lincoln.

- Lost his job – 1832
- First defeat as a legislator – 1832
- Bankrupted – 1833
- Defeated for Speaker – 1838
- Defeated for Congress – 1843
- Lost even the nomination bid for Congress – 1848
- Defeated for the Senate – 1954
- Lost the Vice Presidential nomination – 1856
- Again defeated for the Senate – 1958
- Elected President of the USA – 1860

Cut the crap

A man was driving recklessly. A patrol car overtook him and screeched across, forcing him to brake. A breath test was demanded. The guy replies: "I can't do that. I am an asthmatic and blowing into your machine might trigger off a major asthmatic attack." The cop then asks him to come to the police station for a blood test.

The smart guy is ready: "Sorry Sir. I can't do that. I am a hemophilic and would bleed to death."

The cop then demands a urine sample.

The smart guy has one for that too: "But sorry Sir. I can't do that either. I am a diabetic and if I empty my bladder, my blood sugar would drop down and I would faint."

> *Survivors cut the crap and get to the point straightaway. Acting over-smart is fit only for a laugh in the films. Real life is different. If you beat around the bush, all you would do is raise dust.*

Cop: "OK. In that case why don't you please step out of the car and walk on this straight line for me?"

Smart guy: "I can't do that either!"

Cop: "Why not?" Smart guy: "Because I am drunk!"

Optimal capacity

A man had a goose that laid golden eggs. Everyday it would lay an egg. But this person was greedy. He was not satisfied with one egg a day, and he did not want to kill the goose to get all the eggs in one go either as he had already read the old story.

He contacted a consultant who suggested him to approach a goose expert who told him that he could administer some hormones to make the goose give two eggs a day instead of its usual one.

He spent a fortune on the hormones needed for this and when appropriate doses were administered, he found that it did give two eggs but both were half the size. The man was disappointed and went back to the goose specialist once again. The scientist told him that if he spent some more money he would modify the medicines to produce more eggs.

> *If you try to bend rules to extract more, either the quality will suffer or the machine will suffer a break-down.*

The next day, the goose started giving eggs every five minutes till it gave a hundred eggs. The only problem was that each egg was the size of a mustard grain. In industrial terms, it is called optimal capacity.

Each machine, operation, act or individual has an optimal capacity.

PEARL 88

Doing a favour

We are all asked favours. We are all requested things. On most occasions we agree to help or offer assistance. But only when we actually start doing the thing we know the real extent of trouble that we have to undertake! This funny story illustrates the point.

A persistent and loud knocking at the door disturbed a couple who was fast asleep. The husband looked at the wall clock. It was 3.00 a.m. Lightning was crashing outside while rains lashed incessantly. Wondering as to who the visitor could be, the sleepy eyed husband staggered to the door where he saw a drunk soaking wet, with water dribbling from his raincoat.

> Do a favour by all means but don't let anyone take advantage of you.

"I need a push! I need a push!" he said in a slurred voice.

The husband looked out at the lashing rains. He then looked at the dripping drunk.

"Sorry mate! Try someone else," he said as he snapped the door shut and walked back. He told his wife what had happened and she chided him, "Honey! Haven't you read your Bible? Do to others as you expect others to do to you. Don't you remember our trip last month? If the villagers had not helped us in the middle of the night, won't we have been stuck? It is foul of you not to have helped the stranger!"

Suitably admonished, the husband got up. He spent five minutes wearing a raincoat and a hat. Collecting his torch he walked out into the torrential rain.

"Hey mister! Where are you? I have come to give you a push!"

"Here! This way. In the garden!" came a slurred voice.

He focussed the torch and saw the stranger sitting on a garden swing, waiting for his push.

Ignorance is not bliss

Santa Singh was travelling by ship. He was allotted a berth opposite a Frenchman. The first day they sat for lunch opposite each other, the Frenchman stood up, lifted his hat, bowed a little and said, "Bon Apetit." Santa Singh did not understand the gesture but stood up, lifted his turban, bent his head and said in a loud voice, "Santa Singh."

This was repeated for a few days. Eventually Santa was told by someone that 'Bon Apetit' was a French greeting wishing you a good appetite and a pleasant meal.

The next morning, before the Frenchman could stand up, Santa was on his feet, turban out, head bowed and said, "Bon Apetit."

Lifting his hat, the Frenchman haltingly said, "S-A-N-T-A S-I-N-G-H!"

Many times in real life, we face instructions or situations which we do not understand fully.

> *In such situations, it is best to press the pause button immediately and ask for clarifications. Even if the senior frowns at you, make it clear that it is better to seek clarifications early than to make an ass of yourself later by messing up something.*

The above is applicable in the corporate world too. We have a complex array of thoughts in our mind but sometimes words are a poor medium to communicate exactly what we want.

Value thy freedom

Communism may have its own advantages but human rights is not one of them. The horrors and tortures during the erstwhile Russian regimen has produced a lot of funny stories about the police state under a communist regimen. One goes like this:

A Frenchman, an American and a Russian were discussing happiness. Each had his own definition of the word.

> *Survivors value freedom and cherish it because there is nothing more valuable than it.*

The Frenchman said, "When you are away for the whole month and then come back home and find your girlfriend anxiously waiting at the airport, the tight hug she gives you is real happiness."

The American disagreed and retorted, "In my case the example is a little different. If you have bought a shoe which is one size too tight and then get stuck in a meeting for a long time, the sensation you get when you come home, remove your shoes and wriggle your toes is true happiness!"

The Russian spoke in a soft voice: "You are both wrong. Imagine a scenario when you are sleeping peacefully with your wife. In the dead of the night, you hear sharp knuckles pounding on the door. "Igor – open up! It is the Secret Police," you hear a rough voice. And then if you say – "Sorry! Igor lives next door!" then you are definitely the happiest man on this earth!

In a similar vein, another story goes like this:

A French surgeon, a British surgeon and a Russian surgeon met at a conference. Over drinks, the conversation started about difficult and complex surgical operations. The Frenchman described the complex surgery he had done on a beating heart, which had taken him six hours.

The Englishman shared his experiences by describing a complex brain tumour, which he had removed and which had taken him seven hours. Finally, it was the Russian's turn. He was softspoken and was not dramatic. He said in a matter of fact voice:

"In our country, tonsillectomy is a difficult operation and takes about nine to ten hours on an average!"

The other two surgeons were justifiably surprised. Ten hours for a tonsil removal? It intrigued them and they sought further clarifications.

"Have you tried to remove the tonsils by a rectal approach?" asked the Russian surgeon.

Obviously, in a police state you are not allowed to open your mouth and to operate on tonsils, you have to take an alternative approach! Now that the regimen has gone and Russia has split, the above stories remain as humorous incidents from the past.

PEARL 91 A cheap thing is not always a bargain

This is a true life story that happened to me many years ago. It is a hunting story, but before you skip to the next chapter, let me assure you that there is absolutely no violence in it. This story carries a 'U' Certificate and can be read by everyone.

About ten years ago, I was bitten by a hunting bug. I was told that a shotgun was the best weapon for a beginner. Unlike a rifle which fires a single bullet and needs an accurate aim, a shotgun discharges numerous pellets. Just point and shoot was likely to get you some target. I spent a lot of money and purchased a William Evans Shotgun. The forest ranger who sold me his weapon told me that Evans had worked under 'Birdie' the world's best shotgun makers before he started his own unit.

I was impressed with the weapon and bought it on the spot. I took to rabbit hunting which remained an interesting pastime for many years. And then came ammunition shortage. My weapon's license allowed me to buy two hundred cartridges at one time and all twelve-bore cartridges in our country come from the Indian Ordinance Factory. This factory catered to both the defence and the civil needs and would occasionally stop manufacturing twelve-bore cartridges for months together.

> A survivor looks for the best bargain—the best bargain is not synonymous with the cheapest bargain.

The list price for an IOF 12-bore cartridge is rupees eighteen, but during shortages it would go up to a hundred rupees. Sometimes even when you are willing to pay a premium, you would find that there are no stocks. The only other option was to buy imported rounds. But due to high import duties and restrictions, a Winchester 12-bore cartridge cost two hundred rupees. Rabbit meat was about sixty rupees a kilo and thus it was unwise to spend two hundred rupees for a single round. It was at this time that a friend offered to reload my empties for ten rupees each.

I had a box full of empties and was pleased at having located such an economical source. The first time I used a reloaded cartridge was also possibly my last. This is what happened to me on that day. It was about 8.00 p.m. and we were in my open top jeep. The driver drove, the guide flashed a spotlight and I stood on the back seat with a shotgun on my shoulder looking every bit of Jim Corbett. Only the bowler was missing. And then we saw the rabbit. He was a huge fellow. As big as a big pup. White face with a white, brown and black body. The light caught its eyes and it froze. My shotgun was pointed towards it (not aimed! No sights on a Evans!) and the first trigger pressed. The bang was twice as loud as it would have been with a factory cartridge. A gush of smoke exited out of the barrel and the air was permeated with a sulphurous smell. The bolt shook with a recoil. I waited for the smoke to clear and looked into the bush where our spotlight had caught the rabbit.

To my great surprise, the chap was totally unhurt. He blinked his eyes and quivered his moustache as he stared at me. My reflexes were quick and I squeezed the other barrel, which was not choked. This time I could hear a louder sound, and actually see a flash exit my barrel like in a Second World War movie. The smoke took longer to clear but when it did, the sight startled me.

My only regret was that I did not have a video camera but I have visualised the scene a thousand times in my mental DVD. The rabbit was still there. Its eyes were still on me. Only its moustache was singed and face black with coal and soot. It shook its body, gave a disdainful look and slowly hopped away.

I realised that if you expect a ten-rupee product to perform like a three-hundred-rupee one, you are in for a surprise!

PEARL 92

The company you keep

After he got the Nobel Prize, Einstein was busy with a lecture circuit throughout the US. Incidentally, he had a driver who had a shaggy beard and snow white unruly hair just like him. Every time Einstein gave a lecture, the driver would be seated in the last seat in the auditorium.

One day, while they were driving towards a college, the chauffer turned to him and said, "I have heard this lecture so many times that I could give it better than you!" Einstein laughed and decided to try it out at the next venue.

> *Joke apart, it is a fact that one benefits immensely from the company of people who are more experienced and more knowledgeable than you. Something good is sure to rub off on to you.*

The chauffer was introduced as Einstein and he proceeded to give a lecture on the theory of relativity while Einstein sat in the back row. Surprisingly, he spoke really well and the audience gave him an enthusiastic round of applause. Finally came the question and answer session. At the very outset someone asked a difficult question. Unhesitatingly, the driver said, "Ha! This is such a simple question that even my chauffer can answer it," and pointed towards Einstein in the back row.

Even a dumb person imbibes knowledge if he stays constantly with someone intelligent and knowledgeable. A cotton string used to make a jasmine garland starts smelling as sweet as the flowers themselves.

Smartness pays

In Punjab, Madhya Pradesh, Uttar Pradesh and Bihar, a buffalo is a precious commodity. All buffaloes are black but it needs an expert to distinguish the various shades of grey that lead to an absolute black. Buffalo lovers know that the blacker the buffalo, the more the milk yield. Darker the skin, better the pedigree. Thus it was not unusual for a coal jet black buffalo to be priced significantly higher than its less darker counterpart.

Godrej and Boyce is a famous Indian company that introduced a hair dye for the Indian market. Its single use black hair dye sachets costing rupees ten were sold with a marketing slogan of *Kato-Kholo-Gholo-Lagao*. Snip, mix, dissolve apply. And all your grey hair gone. When the product was launched, the marketing guys predicted a greater sale in the urban areas and projected the four metropolitan cities as the ideal target markets. But after a year when the sales figures were tallied, it turned out that the maximum sales occurred in the rural areas of Punjab, Madhya Pradesh, Uttar Pradesh and Bihar. It was much later that the company would know that twenty sachets would increase a buffalo's value by a third!

> *Human mind and enterprise finds solutions to the most seemingly impossible problems*

Thus sachets of Godrej permanent hair dye, which were originally designed to darken human hair, found use for darkening the buffaloes because though it did not increase the milk yield, it decidedly made the buffaloes glisten in their black glory.

PEARL 94 — Don't hide anything from your doctor and lawyer

A man went to a doctor. The doctor told him that he had procured a new computerised machine which would do a single urine test and diagnose all his problems. The patient was not convinced but agreed to return to collect his report. The next day he was told that the machine had diagnosed the problem as a case of Tennis Elbow. The man was angry! He told the physician that he was not satisfied with the diagnosis. The doctor reassured him and said, "Oh don't worry. I will repeat this test for you. I won't charge you anything. Here, take this bottle and get me a sample."

As the chap drove home with the bottle, he was getting irritated by the way in which computers and machines are taking over our lives. He decided to play a prank on the doctor's computer. He collected his sample. He then asked his wife and daughter to mix their samples in it. Then he added a little engine oil from his car and shook the bottle vigorously to mix the contents thoroughly.

> *Never lie to your doctor or lawyer or conceal information from them. If you have reposed confidence in them, repose it fully. They will be able to make a proper diagnosis or prepare a proper defence only if they have all the facts right before them. Later don't blame them for wrong diagnosis or a jail sentence.*

He had a naughty smile on his face as he entered the doctor's chamber the next day. The doctor looked at him and said, "You have no reason to smile like this. You are in deep trouble. Your wife has gonorrhea, your teenaged daughter is pregnant, your car needs overhauling and if you don't stop shaking the bottle like this, your tennis elbow will never get better!"

PEARL 95: At the end of everything, there is God

Shah Jehan, the great Mogul emperor, had a compulsive obsession of recovering the land of his forefathers in Central Asia, and mounted three campaigns there to capture Qandahar. The first two were led by Aurangzeb, then a Prince. When he was unsuccessful, Shah Jehan sent his favourite son Dara Shikoh, having given him the exalted title of Shah Buland Iqbal (King of Lofty Fortunes).

Dara besieged the fort of Qandahar with a seventy-thousand strong army and in fact ran over a nearby place called Bist. Victory appeared to be in sight after all. Dara was elated but being the sophisticated man that he was, he composed a poem and sent it to the Persian fort commander Autar Khan, asking him to surrender and threatened him with a massacre if he refused.

> *Survivors never forsake their faith in God.*

The reply which the redoubtable Autar Khan gave in the form of a couplet has become historic and has inspired generations of faithfuls since then: **"Let the sword of the entire world move, it would not cut a blade of grass if God does not will it."**

The Moguls were indeed obliged to lift the seize after 157 days when, amusingly enough, they ran out of ammunition. Qandahar was to remain unconquered, a castle that really laughed a siege to scorn!

Kindness

It is not always necessary to expect something in return while we offer help. It is also not necessary to spend either time or money to help someone. All it needs is the mental will and some physical effort.

A friend of mine had gone to Besant Nagar beach and found an elderly couple walking along slowly. The wife seemed to be limping and the elderly husband supported her as she walked ahead. My friend looked at them and was somehow impelled to say a 'hello' and start talking with them. It turned out that though the couple were affluent and had a son working in the US, they were lonely. They invited him for a cup of coffee and my friend accompanied them. He found that the old couple were really lonely. They did not lack comforts or luxuries. Their son had stocked the house with all the latest luxuries and labour saving devices, nevertheless, even their new DVD player lay boxed and unopened.

> *A small gesture can result in happiness for both—the giver as well as the recipient.*

My friend surprised them on the next Friday by picking up a few DVDs of old mythological movies and the three of them spent a joyous afternoon which was one of the many to come. My friend had lost his parents in his childhood and the elderly couple were missing their son who was abroad. My friend found his parents in the older couple, while they found a son in him. A simple act of kindness got them both a wonderful relationship.

A pig remains a pig

A farmer in rural England had a guest for dinner. While they were being served, they saw a pig totter around with a wooden leg. On three good legs and a wooden leg he looked both pitiable and funny. The guest asked:

"Why does this pig have a wooden leg?"

The farmer became a little thoughtful as he said, "Well, you see, we have had him for the last six years and he has sort of become a family to us. A few year ago when our youngest son fell down into the swimming pool, it was this pig which jumped into the pool and rescued him!"

"Oh! So the pig lost its leg in the swimming accident, is it?"

No! no! That came later. The next year we were all sleeping when a fire broke out in the barn. Before it could spread all over and consume us, this piggy went to the main console and broke the glass to press the fire alarm."

> *Obviously, the first impressions last till the end. A pig remains a pig, no matter how exceptionally it performs.*

"Oh! I see. So he lost his leg in the fire accident."

"No! no! That came later. Two years ago he started digging in the rear yard of our house. He dug and dug, and suddenly something black sprang out. We later found out that it was an oil well and that is what has made us multi-millionaires!"

"But you never said how the pig broke his leg, or how he came to have a wooden leg?"

"Well, such a special pig, you don't eat at all once, do you?"

Lateral effect

A millionaire wanted to get rid of his wife but did not want to divorce her because he wanted to save on the alimony. He consulted his adviser and a lawyer, who told him to buy her a single engine plane and teach her to fly. She would surely die in a plane crash. Three months later the distraught husband called the lawyer and told his that not only had the wife turned out to be an excellent pilot but had also won the first prize in the Aerial Acrobatics competition.

> *In management terms, we call it lateral effect. The consequences of misunderstanding can produce surprising developments.*

After a lot of thought, the lawyer advised him to get the wife a horse and teach her riding. She would fall off the horse and break her neck. Three months later the anxious husband informed his counsel that not only had she become an excellent jockey but had also won a few championship races. The lawyer wanted a few days to think over his next plan. He checked the Internet and found out that automobile accidents were the commonest cause of death in developed countries. He called the husband and said:

"Buy your wife a jaguar. Let us see what happens this time!"

The next day a happy and enthusiastic husband thanked his lawyer effusively on the phone. When the lawyer asked for details, the husband said:

"This morning when she went to feed the jaguar, it bit her head off!"

Alcohol

Father James was a popular pastor who gave convincing sermons. Mrs. Smith lamented that Mr. Smith was an incurable alcoholic and used to find a new excuse each time for his vigorous drinking bouts. The priest agreed to give his Sunday sermon on the ills of alcohol and Mrs. Smith promised to get Mr. Smith along.

Father James wanted to make a dramatic presentation and thus he faced his flock with a jar full of live earthworms, a bottle of whisky, a jug of water and two empty glasses. In full view of his congregation, he filled one glass with whisky and the other with water. Picking up a couple of wriggling live earthworms he dropped one into each. In two minutes, the earthworm in the whisky glass was floating up dead while the one in clear water was swimming majestically. Father James summoned Mr. Smith to the podium and asked "Well Mr. Smith! What does this prove to you?"

> *An addict will always find ways and means to satisfy his cravings.*

"Passshtor!" slurred Smith.

"If you want wormsh to grow in your stomach, drink water. If you want to kill them, drink whisky!"

Formal education is not the same as knowledge

𝒫etticoat Street in London had a church called Saint James Rectory. Some archaic and ancient church rules mandatorised that the church would not employ anyone without formal education. At least a basic high school education was a must. Alfred Dunhill was a caretaker whose job was to clean the pew, sweep the floor and keep the podium spick and span. The old pastor was benign and not a stickler of rules. Dunhill lacked formal education and had put off to taking his high school examination till it became too late.

Once the old priest retired, he was replaced by a younger person who was a lot stricter and followed the rule book. Looking through the records, he found that Dunhill had not completed his schooling. The pastor called the caretaker and ordered a notice. Either he gets a high school certificate in six months or he tenders his resignation. A distraught Dunhill knew that you could not teach an old dog new tricks and that he had no option but to resign.

He started out on his afternoon stroll immersed in deep thought. He got into Bond Street and was suddenly seized by an urge to smoke. He kept looking to his side while he walked the entire length of Bond Street and could not find a single tobacconist. He had to walk further down into a side street to locate a shop where he purchased his cigarette.

Back again on the busy Bond Street, as he puffed his cigarette and saw the milling crowd, he realised that a small cigarette shop in the street would be a sound business proposition. He resigned his job and started a small shop which succeeded way beyond his expectations. Dunhill's eyes glanced across the street and realised that a lot of people had walked all around the road from the other side to come to him. He started another small shop on the opposite side of Bond Street.

Business was better than expected and the two shops multiplied to four and then sixteen. In three years, Alfred Dunhill & Company was a leading tobacconist of England. He started machine-rolling cigarettes and introduced his own brand of Dunhill cigarettes. In five years he was a millionaire many times over. To ensure a consistent supply of tobacco, he entered into an annual purchase agreement with a couple of American tobacco farmers, to meet whom he went to America.

It was a big boost for the American tobacco formers and the contract signing ceremony was converted into a media circus with a Senator and Governor participating. When the contracts were actually signed, Dunhill affixed his thumb impression because he had not learnt to sign his name. The Governor was impressed and said,

> *Fools say they learn by their own experience; I prefer to learn from others' experiences.*

"Well Sir! This is awesome. Even without a formal education you have achieved so much. Just imagine what you would have done if you had a formal education!"

Dunhill's characteristic oft repeated reply was: "If I knew to read and write, I would still be sweeping the rectory!"

I|MPUS001|2021|05|07